Will Henry / Clay Fisher
(Henry W. Allen)

Twayne's United States Authors Series

Warren French, Editor

Indiana University, Indianapolis

TUSAS 466

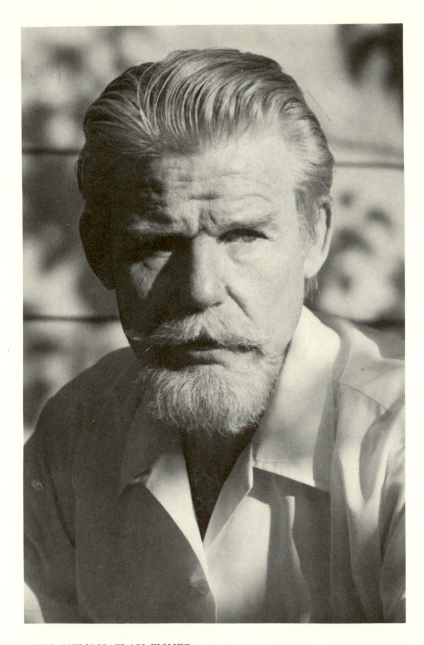

WILL HENRY/CLAY FISHER
(HENRY W. ALLEN)
Photograph courtesy of Bruce Gaylor, Encino

Will Henry / Clay Fisher
(Henry W. Allen)

By Robert L. Gale

University of Pittsburgh

Twayne Publishers • *Boston*

Will Henry/Clay Fisher
(Henry W. Allen)

Robert L. Gale

Copyright © 1984 by G. K. Hall & Company
All Rights Reserved
Published by Twayne Publishers
A Division of G. K. Hall & Company
70 Lincoln Street
Boston, Massachusetts 02111

Book Production by Marne B. Sultz

Book Design by Barbara Anderson

Printed on permanent/durable acid-free
paper and bound in the United States of
America.

Library of Congress Cataloging in Publication Data

Gale, Robert L.
      Will Henry/Clay Fisher (Henry W. Allen)

      (Twayne's United States authors series: TUSAS 466)
      Bibliography: p. 143
      Includes index.
      1. Henry, Will, 1912–   —Criticism and interpretation.
2. Western stories—History and criticism.
3. Indians in literature.   I. Title.   II. Series.
PS3551.L393Z68   1984   813'.54   83-18255
ISBN 0-8057-7407-6

To Will
(Henry Wilson Allen)
My Best Western Friend
The Slightly Better Half of Will & Clay
The Far Better Half of Will & Bob

Contents

About the Author

Robert Lee Gale was born in Des Moines, Iowa, and was educated at Dartmouth College (B.A.) and Columbia University (M.A. and Ph.D.). He served in the U.S. Army Counter-Intelligence Corps in Europe during World War II. He has taught at Columbia, the University of Delaware, the University of Mississippi, and the University of Pittsburgh, where he is now professor of American Literature. He has had Fulbright teaching fellowships to Italy and Finland, and has also lectured in Germany, Canada, Denmark, and Russia. Gale is the author of *The Caught Image: Figurative Language in the Fiction of Henry James; Thomas Crawford, American Sculptor; Plots and Characters in Henry James*, and in *Nathaniel Hawthorne, Herman Melville, Edgar Allan Poe*, and *Mark Twain*; the "Henry James" chapter in *Eight American Authors* (revised edition); Western Writers Series booklets *Charles Warren Stoddard, Charles Marion Russell*, and *Will Henry/Clay Fisher*; and many study guides, chapters and articles in reference works, critical essays, and reviews. He is currently editing the *Plots and Characters Series*, which to date numbers fifteen volumes. Gale is the author of the TUSAS volumes on *Richard Henry Dana, Jr., Francis Parkman, John Hay*, and *Luke Short*. He teaches courses in American literature, especially nineteenth-century fiction, Civil War literature, the Roaring Twenties, and Western literature.

Preface

The name Henry Wilson Allen is virtually unknown to lovers of modern Western fiction. But under his two pen names, Will Henry and Clay Fisher, Henry W. Allen has published more than fifty books, which have sold in excess of 15,000,000 copies, give or take a ton. Many have been made into splendid movies. Allen is still productive, and his books continue to sell well. He has been in print with Bantam Books for thirty-two consecutive years, in itself a remarkable tribute.

Allen has been a major influence on a number of outstanding writers of Western fiction. Thomas Berger comes to mind as having borrowed from and built upon the historomantic style of Allen. Others of similar skills and reputations, indeed practically a generation of younger Western writers, have "gone to school" to the works of Will Henry and Clay Fisher. Allen has won at least ten prestigious awards and is considered by many practicing Western writers as the best nontraditional Western fiction writer now alive.

Why, then, is Allen so persistently underrated and neglected by critics?

To a degree, most Western writers are played down by Eastern Establishment reviewers and commentators. But the matter is deeper than that. Allen is unique. That is his trouble. He writes for an audience of one—Allen. He is also shy, private. He has never advanced himself by way of television talk shows and the like. In a way, he is the B. Traven of the Far and the Old West. But the matter goes still deeper. Allen has taken the Indian side of "history," and much of his best work is therefore a rebuke to the white Establishment—military and otherwise—especially when it comes to telling about Custer, Crazy Horse, Sitting Bull, Red Beard Crook, One Hand Howard, Bear Coat Miles, Preacher Chivington, Black Kettle, Chief Joseph, Dull Knife, Little Wolf, the Apache Kid, Juh, Geronimo, Chato, Jesse James, Wyatt Earp, Henry Plummer, Isom Dart, Butch Cassidy, Tom Horn, and Teddy Roosevelt—among others. But the result is revisionist historomance without parallel in its steady brilliance.

WILL HENRY/CLAY FISHER (HENRY W. ALLEN)

In addition to adopting two pen names, a decision which he now regrets, Allen decided early not to write simply about the clash of Indians and their white betrayers west of the Missouri River. He also has written about cowboys and trail drivers, rustlers and whiskey runners, road agents and vigilantes, horse thieves and hanging posses, gunmen and gold miners, escaped slaves and army deserters, prison-breakers and bounty hunters—and animals. And books for children. And books about the Civil War, and the Spanish-American War, and the Alaskan Gold Rush, and the Texas Rangers. And, under his own name, fiction set in contemporary times and, for good measure, in the twenty-first century. All of this versatility is tied together by four unifying strands: authenticity, humor, excitement, and literary artistry.

Two distinguished parallels from the middle of America's nine-teenth century commend themselves for consideration. Allen does with Western history and legend what Nathaniel Hawthorne did with the story of Merrymount's famous Maypole and what Herman Melville did with Israel Potter, Benito Cereno, and the Spithead and Nore mutinies—that is, converts authentic event into narrative yarn. And two later American novelists suggest themselves as analogues also. Allen has the wild, critical humor and the dark passion of Mark Twain and William Faulkner. I realize that I am thus placing Allen in very serious literary company—because just possibly that is where he belongs.

After a brief first chapter on Henry Allen's life, this book has chapters on Henry/Fisher fiction dealing with Sioux, Crow, Cheyenne, Mandan, Shoshone, Nez Percé, Comanche, and Apache Indians, usually in their gallant, bloody, hopeless conflict with the American army (chapters 2 and 3); with horsemen of various kinds, on the cattle trail and on the run (chapter 4); gunmen good and bad (chapter 5); Civil War (and later) soldiers, sometimes as menaced by Indians in the Deep Southwest as by each other, and fanatics seeking gold mines, often lost to mortal view (chapter 6). Then comes a critical miscellany on Allen's short stories, his books for children, his con-temporary-scene and sci-fi futuristic works, and his literary criticism (chapter 7). Then some comments on Allen's style and his message to us (chapter 8).

What started for me as pleasant off-duty reading of stray Henrys and Fishers turned quickly into a valued part of my Western American literature course here at Pitt. Then came the idea of trying to interest a publisher or two in a study of Allen. After some false leads and rebukes, I won a yes from the editors of the Western Writers Series, Boise State University, Boise, Idaho, and wrote a pamphlet entitled *Will Henry/Clay Fisher* as part of that fine series. Neither the Boise people nor the editors of G. K. Hall and Company, Boston, objected to my expanding my insights on Allen into a volume for Twayne's U.S. Authors Series, to follow my TUSAS *Luke Short.*

I shall always be grateful to everyone concerned with my Allen project. In the first place, it was fun to read the more than 10,000 pages of published material by Allen. It was never dull; rather, it became addictive. Allen is a master storyteller. Often I started reading another Allen title ten minutes after finishing a previous one. In the second place, reading Allen sent me to some of his historical and background sources, and the result was always surprising, illuminating, educative, humbling. There was—and of course is—so very much background material that I was ignorant of, and still am. An alleged well-wisher once wrote me that I could not qualify as an expert until I had read 6,000 books on the West, the way he and his collaborator had done. I confess that I have not yet reached that total. But I have been trying. Best of all, in the third place, I got to know Henry Allen—and to admire him almost as a character from one of his own novels. I wrote him care of the Screen Writers' Guild, Los Angeles, on August 27, 1979. His characteristically modest and engaging reply started it all. Since that date our correspondence has grown to more than 275 letters. Mine are querulous. His are generous and captivating. Without his help this study could not have been. As my annotations reveal, it is a joint effort.

To other friends I owe a debt of gratitude as well. I especially thank Clarence Decater, book collector, Roseville, California; David H. Elder, artist, University of Pittsburgh, Pittsburgh, Pennsylvania; Richard W. Etulain, historian, critic, editor, University of New Mexico, Albuquerque, New Mexico; Warren French, critic, editor, Indiana—Purdue University, Indianapolis, Indiana; Brian Garfield, Western author, Hollywood, California; Edward Kemp, archivist, University of Oregon, Eugene, Oregon; James H. Maguire, critic, editor, Boise State University, Boise, Idaho; Dwight Newton, Western writer, Bend, Oregon; Russel Nye, critic, University of Michigan, Ann Arbor, Michi-

WILL HENRY/CLAY FISHER (HENRY W. ALLEN)

gan; David S. Sims, Western writer, on the loose; C. L. Sonnichsen, historian nonpareil, Tucson, Arizona; Jon Tuska, critic, Milwaukie, Oregon; and Dale L. Walker, Western author, critic, editor, University of Texas at El Paso. It is fashionable for an author to thank his mentors and friends for their help but then to add that lingering mistakes in his work are his doing. But I must say that some of my above-named friends led me astray and that several of the excellences —not all, mind you—of my Allen book are my own responsibility.

Robert L. Gale

University of Pittsburgh

Chronology

1912   Henry Wilson Allen, Jr. ("Will Henry," "Clay Fisher") born September 29 in Kansas City, Missouri, third of five children (Audrey, Robert, Henry, Bruce, and Sherris) of Dr. Henry Wilson Allen, Sr. (1881–1953) and Ella Jensen Allen (1884–1960).

1930   Graduated from Southwest High School, Kansas City; traveled in California, the Southwest, Mexico; resolved to live in the West permanently; attended Kansas City Polytechnic Institute three terms (until 1932).

1932   Worked in gold mines at Ward and Jamestown, Colorado (until spring 1933).

1934   Returned to California to stay; worked as writer in film studios.

1937   Married Amy Geneva Watson (stage name "Dorothy Hope") in Hollywood, California (two children: Valerie Hope Allen [Brasher], 1942; Christopher Bruce Allen, 1945).

1938   Worked as contract writer of short subjects for Metro-Goldwyn-Mayer, Culver City, California (until 1941).

1942   Declared exempt from military service because of eardrum perforation; worked on army training films at MGM (until 1945).

1945   Returned to writing MGM short subjects (to 1949).

1950   Published first "Will Henry" novel (*No Survivors*).

1951   Published first "Clay Fisher" novel (*Red Blizzard*) and first book for children (*Wolf-Eye* [Will Henry]).

1955   Established residence in Encino, California; obtained first contract for feature-film writing, 20th Century Fox (first draft of screenplay of *The Tall Men*, with Clark Gable); first movies based on his fiction released (*The Tall Men* and *Santa Fe Passage*).

1960   Received Western Writers of America Spur Award for best historical novel of the year, and won first annual Levi Strauss

Golden Saddleman (both for *From Where the Sun Now Stands*).

1962   Won WWA Spur Award for best short story of the year ("Isley's Stranger"); published first collection of short stories (*The Oldest Maiden Lady in New Mexico*).

1963   Won WWA Spur Award for best historical novel of the year (*The Gates of the Mountains*).

1965   Won WWA Spur Award for best short story of the year ("The Tallest Indian in Toltepec").

1966   Published second major short-story collection (*Sons of the Western Frontier*).

1967   Won WWA special award for "fine writing of the American West" (*One More River to Cross*).

1968   Won WWA special award for "fine writing of the American West" (*Alias Butch Cassidy*); most successful movie based on his fiction released (*Mackenna's Gold*, with Gregory Peck and Omar Sharif).

1970   Received Outstanding Service Award, National Cowboy Hall of Fame.

1972   Received Western Heritage Wrangler Award, National Cowboy Hall of Fame, and won WWA Spur Award for best historical novel of the year (both for *Chiricahua*).

1975   Won Border Regional Library Association (Texas) Fiction Award "for literary excellence and enrichment of the cultural heritage of the Southwest" (*I, Tom Horn*).

1983   Published third major short-story collection (*Seven Legends West*); Bantam estimates 15,000,000 Henry and Fisher books sold.

Chapter One

Life and Works

One day in 1949 a young Metro-Goldwyn-Mayer short-subject script writer was caught by alleged superiors in his Culver City company office writing a novel on company time. He was fired but did not reform. Instead, he continued to resist honest 9-to-5 toil all he could, and continued to produce fiction. After all, the suddenly exposed novel was not his first but *Red Blizzard*, his second. His first, *No Survivors*, had already been accepted by Random House, although it was not yet in print. The young man completed his second book on his penurious own, and he has been independent and happy at his trade of historomancing (though not too penurious) ever since. Being caught was the turning point of his life.

Will Henry or Clay Fisher?

Our unabashed short-subject writer was Henry Wilson Allen. Or was he? His first novel, *No Survivors*, is signed by "Will Henry," but his second, *Red Blizzard*, is by "Clay Fisher." The explanation only seems simple. While Allen was on MGM contract, that company with the big lion's mouth regarded all of his writing as their exclusive property. Hence the pen name Will Henry. Allen then as always had a brain teeming with ideas for novels. So it should surprise no one to learn that before *No Survivors* could see print he had several more books planned. Once the editors at Random House had accepted both *No Survivors* (published in 1950) and *To Follow a Flag* (1953; retitled *Pillars of the Sky*, 1956), they did not wish to commit themselves to Allen's next two books, already nearing completion. Hence the second name, Clay Fisher, not only for *Red Blizzard* (which Simon and Schuster published in 1951) but also for *Santa Fe Passage* (sold to Houghton Mifflin and published in 1953). Incredibly, between the time *Red Blizzard* and *Santa Fe Passage* had been contracted for and the time they were published, Allen had completed *Yellow*

Hair and *Warbonnet*, both as Clay Fisher and both published in 1953 by Houghton Mifflin; in addition, Allen as Will Henry saw into print the first of his five excellent books for children—*Wolf-Eye: The Bad One* (1951, Julian Messner).

The question of the two pen names became a vexing one. Allen wrote me to explain that "after the first two or three titles at Random House and Houghton Mifflin, the Will Henry and Clay Fisher names were well set in their separate but parallel courses, and remained that way" (A to G, 1/5/81). Part of the time, he used to feel that his two selves were distinct. He wrote me thus: "I am unique among western authors, I believe, by wide margin, in having owned and operated two authors, each working at a separate level, and successful at the two levels, for thirty years" (A to G, 4/11/80). Only one critic, Anne Falke, has attempted to distinguish in detail a Henry novel from a Fisher. She valuably notes the following:

> The Fisher novels employ a more typically "Western" form. The narrative follows a more direct and unified course, avoiding the greater number of characters and episodic structure that is typical of the Henry style. Fishers run a hundred pages shorter on the average [not so] and cover a much shorter period of time. Many of them . . . cover only two or three days. Some . . . occur over a few months, but use a single, bare action line. The Henry books cover years . . . and as a rule avoid the central incident or limited problem that commonly forms the frame for a Clay Fisher book.[1]

Falke also contrasts the typical Fisher hero, who is formulaic and unitary, with the typical Henry hero, who is complex and more conscious of history.[2] On the other hand, a pair of critics, Jon Tuska and Vicki Piekarski, too hastily generalize that "Henry Allen . . . uses the Fisher pen name for his more formulary efforts."[3]

All three critics just named fail to take into consideration the fact that Fisher and Henry often galloped within hailing distance of each other. Thus, Allen now defines *The Brass Command*, a Fisher novel published in 1956, as properly a Henry, and *Summer of the Gun*, a Henry novel published in 1978, as a Fisher, and adds that "not all of my books came out under the proper penname . . . Perhaps three or four others got into print under the wrong name" (A to G, 1/29/82). Further, *Red Blizzard* (Fisher) retells aspects of *No Survivors* (Henry), while *The Last Warpath* (Henry, 1966) reworks sizable parts of *No Survivors, Yellow Hair* (Fisher), and *The Brass*

Command. One reviewer half-accused Allen of plagiarizing from himself in his *Last Warpath*.[4] All of this bothers the novelist not a whit. He has remarked, "I am an 'experimentalist.' The cross-pollinating of plotlines and characters is something I had fun with. If it helped, . . . great. I often work on these books . . . in a sort of sealed-off earth of my own, wherein I *do* tell the stories to titillate myself."[5]

The fact that Henry and Fisher, seemingly two different writers of Western fiction, were in reality the same person was probably no mystery to innumerable people by the mid-1960s. In 1964 the dust jacket of Fisher's *Valley of the Bear* was touted as "his fifteenth Indian novel; his first for younger readers." But a year later, opposite the title page of Henry's *In the Land of the Mandans* is listed *Valley of the Bear* among other books by Will Henry. So, perhaps wisely, Allen made what he called "a personal choice in 1965 or thereabouts to concentrate on the Will Henry career and let Clay Fisher more or less bump along on his own. This choice [he adds] meant to me that I considered Will Henry the superior of the writers, and I still do" (A to G, 1/5/81).

Here are further complications. Allen wrote an editor-friend, Dale L. Walker, that "[t]he two-names-thing was the worst mistake I was ever to make as a commercial novelist. . . . I would rather take that move back—the two pennames—than any error of my working life. Had I all fifty Will Henry/Clay Fisher novels under one name . . . today, I would be immeasurably the better off professionally and commercially and, indeed, most important of all, historically."[6] This is so, Allen concludes, because although his Henrys seem to display "more substance and seriousness," there is "finally . . . no definable difference" in the fiction of his two pseudonymous selves (A to G, 1/5/81).

To render matters more bewildering, Allen has published two novels with contemporary settings—*Tayopa!* and *See How They Run* (both 1970)—as well as a futuristic science-fiction horror novel, *Genesis Five* (1968), all signed with his real name, presumably to reserve the names Henry and Fisher for his westerns.

I privately suspect that when Allen got an especially fine idea for a novel and then developed it really well, he signed it Henry rather than Fisher. The quality of his Henrys is generally higher than that of his often somewhat hasty Fishers, although obviously there are exceptions. In any event, I propose to treat all of his fiction as if it has proceeded from one fine single mind and ready typewriter—as it has.

Life

The real Henry W. Allen will now please stand up. Henry Wilson Allen was born on September 29, 1912, in Kansas City, Missouri. Originally called Westport Landing, Kansas City was a gateway to the West as much as Pittsburgh, St. Louis, and other key cities were in their various ways. Westport was the eastern jumping-off point for the famed Santa Fe Trail leading through what are now the states of Kansas, Oklahoma, Colorado, and New Mexico to Santa Fe. In his youth Allen must often have thought—as did fellow Missourian Tom Horn—of the dangers and excitements along the old trail "out there."

The Allens are of Scottish and English background. An illustrious Allen back up the family tree was Ethan Allen, one of the Green Mountain Boys and later a hero of the American Revolution. The novelist writes of his father, Dr. H. Wilson Allen, that "Dad was the first oral surgeon in that part of the country, and the Confederate Veterans were a part of his charity caseload. . . . My father . . . treated Cole Younger when he was living out his old age in the home he had bought for a faithful niece, in Lee's Summit, Missouri" (A to G, 4/6/82). Dr. Allen had a well-stocked library, in which young Henry foraged voraciously: ". . . he had the most remarkable wide swings of taste in authors [he says of his father]. He would have shelves of Lytton, Darwin, Chaucer, various Shakespeares, then a spate of Jack London, Bret Hartes, Richard Harding Davises, then more good stuff, Poe, Emerson, Wilde, Thoreau, Macaulay, back to Conan Doyle, Kipling, O. Henry, Twain, about face again to De Maupassant, Scott, Dickens, Tolstoi and Tennyson. . . . He had also a penchant for Robert Louis Stevenson. . . . And . . . 'we' shared a common love and loyalty to the old Tentmaker [Omar Khayyam], Fitzgerald Translation. . . . My favorite [reading] was the Britannica . . ." (A to G, 7/15/81).

Allen's mother Ella Jensen Allen, a gifted portraitist, was of Danish background. His maternal grandfather Allen likens to Anwar Sadat—"including the military bearing and the delightful accent. Grandfather was also a soldier, a member of the King's Guard, in

Denmark. So perhaps all of my heroes are not cowboys, after all" (A to G, 10/7/81).

Allen has two older siblings, Audrey and Robert, and two younger ones, Bruce and Sherris (A to G, 10/13/81). Allen notes that thus he "was the middle one . . . Has been in the middle ever since" (A to G, 3/3/81). After graduating from Southwest High School, in Kansas City, he spent a year and a half in Kansas City Polytechnic Institute (commonly referred to then as "K.C. Junior College"— A to G, 7/20/82). Part of this time his parents urged him to go on and study animal husbandry at the Kansas State Industrial College, at Manhattan, Kansas, or to prepare for a career in journalism by enrolling at the University of Missouri at Columbia (A to G, 1/5/81). But he decided instead to go west, partly because in the spring and at other times young blood urges toward adventures of various sorts. As Allen put it later, "Through the windows in his biology class, he and his fellow students were treated to a full panorama of the local house of ill repute operating around the clock in the adjoining old brick building. This was definitely not the Greatest Little Whorehouse in Kansas City, but it did give young Allen an idea that he was studying biology in the wrong building. Saddling up, he rode west" (A to G, 3/3/81).

"West" during the Great Depression meant for Allen two types of work. He caravaned used cars from the Dust Bowl to California, and he took a variety of jobs "as a journeyman cowhand/sheepherder/horse wrangler/hard rock miner."[7] During one used-car junket "Allen [says Allen] picked up an eighteen-year-old [female] hitchhiker who turned out to be thirteen by the time the caravan had crossed three state lines. The local police in Albuquerque proved sympathetic, even envious, but Allen was returned to Missouri, protesting every mile that he had never laid a glove on the mini-queen and was himself but seventeen." He might have been jailed but for his promise to take an honest job "at $15 per week, six days per week, feeding 100-lb. sacks of raw sugar into a powdered sugar finishing mill."[8]

The West soon called again, and Allen decamped to Colorado, where he spent a winter in the gold fields around Ward and Jamestown, as mucker, blacksmith, driller, and blaster. A premature explosion "disrupted" one of his eardrums, "curing his gold fever" (A to G, 7/11/81), and later forcing him out of military service in World War II.[9] Moving on, "he wandered and worked" the West from New Mexico and Arizona to Montana and Wyoming (A to G, 7/11/81). Eventually, a fractious pack mare—one of seven in a string—threw him and stepped on him "unfriendly in the process," leaving him with a "re-arranged left foot and three cracked ribs," which convinced him that he and the cowboy life "had best part company permanent."[10]

California loomed. Allen defines this region as the land of "$10,000 polo ponies and $1,000,000 movie stars" (A to G, 7/11/81). He soon was at work there, exercising said ponies "for such Hollywood toffs as Walt Disney, Daryll Zanuck, Will Rogers, Snowy Baker and Guinn 'Big Boy' Williams." Soon injured again, Allen began his decade of writing short subjects for MGM, "being hired and fired and rehired five times and/or exactly often enough to destroy his pension eligibility forever." In November 1937 he had married Amy Geneva Watson, a girl from York, Pennsylvania, who happily was a "Busby Berkeley chorus-line lovely" (A to G, 3/3/81) dancing under the stage name of Dorothy Hope. Allen holds that "the whole world runs on luck, and finding my wife was the grandest piece of luck ever to bless one man" (A to G, 4/6/82). The Allens have two children, a daughter Valerie Hope Allen Brasher, born 1942, and a son Christopher Bruce Allen, born 1945.

As already reported, Allen in the late 1940s was not yet a successful novelist. He was still working intermittently as a would-be short-subject film writer. He even tried a brief stint "as a columnist for the *Sunset Reporter*, a 'district' paper in Santa Monica, Calif." (A to G, 1/5/81). He also took a job on the assembly line of the General Motors Chevrolet plant in Van Nuys for $2.53 per hour. His assignment was to carry brutally heavy boxes of steel parts needed along the line. As he objectively reports, "I did not quit . . . They just got tired of stepping over my exhausted body on the floor, and carried me home to my wife in a basket stretcher, complete with good conduct discharge ribbon" (A to G, 4/6/82). Fortunately, *No Survivors* and *Red Blizzard* and all the rest followed. To assure Allen's freedom from 9-to-5 thralldom, fate saw to it that "*Passage* and *Blizzard* and *Flag* all sold to the movies in a few weeks and [Allen goes on] I suddenly had enough money—as I saw it—to buy GM and burn it down."[11]

On their ranch in Van Nuys in the San Fernando Valley, the Allens raised German shepherd show dogs, pedigreed 300-egg Rhode

Island Red chickens, and prize-winning Persian cats. They also fancied Arabian horses and owned the well-known Bell Ranch Quarter mare Francine, which produced several notable show and track winners. In his more active and keener-eyed years Allen also was a licensed American Kennel Commission dog-show judge and a qualified National Rifle Association "Distinguished Expert" with the .45 automatic pistol.[12]

Allen remains devoted to history wherever he lives and whatever else he does. His present Encino home in the foothills of the Santa Monica Mountains, a San Fernando Valley flank of which guards his half-acre *estancia*, is less than half a mile from the ancient Indian hot springs of Los Encinos, where famed Spanish-explorer Gaspar de Portola rested his weary company in 1769, the first white men to camp in the Valley, "a magic place so green," when Portola first saw it, "as to appear planted and cultivated." At the end of Allen's street, five minutes by foot, spreads the fabled Encino Oak, registered No. 24 on the Monument Protection list of the City of Angels, said to have been as old as four hundred years when Portola passed its way. "It still bears its acorns," Allen says, "and the Indian spring still flows its heated waters. Somewhere, old Gaspar is looking down and nodding, yes, I was there. It was the same. It will be the same, also, when you are gone as long as I." And so in this once-lovely, now evilly crowded paradise, Will Henry and Clay Fisher were born, flourished, and wrote great Western prose, "when all about the magic place was yet so green" (A to G, 4/6/82).

Allen believes the beauty of the early California years conspired to lift up the imagination and incline the spirit toward the written word, hence toward his life of storytelling. Of his experiences both before and after he first saw the San Fernando Valley, and germane to his later creativity, Allen has written comprehensively:

... I have wandered the far mesas, whistled up the racing sheepdog, ridden 'round the bedding herd of whitefaced cattle, been "throwed" a mile and twenty minutes by the salty bronco that did not care for the bite of the frosty saddle at four o'clock in the morning, worked nine hundred feet down in the deepshaft Colorado gold mines, flunkied for the post store on Indian reservations, tended rodeo stock, stick-and-balled strings of green polo ponies, pitched sweet prairie hay and likewise sour, stall-strod, straw-manure and, well, just about done what had to be done wherever I was at whatever particular moment of my growing years, boy and man, out in the still-wonderful American West of the early 1930's. And *that* was my motivating factor to write the books I have written. I was there: God couldn't have sent me to wander in a better wilderness, nor enrolled me in a fitter school, to teach me what it was I must write about that others might learn to love the land and is people, and to honor them and their remarkable history, as they really were and not as fabricated on Hollywood celluloid or in the sulphured world of penny-a-word pulpsters.[13]

Allen sounds here a good deal like what he has proved himself to be—a combination of aspects of Walt Whitman, Mark Twain, and Charles Marion Russell. "I was the man, I suffer'd, I was there"— said Whitman. Mark Twain gloried in the variety of his jobs before he became an admired author. And Russell, like Allen and many other Western writers, went to school to nature and preferred the Old West to anything else.

Success

Since 1950 Allen has written with admirable steadiness. On a typical day he "expertly hammers his pre-historic Hermes 3000 portable" (A to G, 4/6/82) from 7:00 A.M. to 6:00 P.M., at his Encino residence, often in a redwood studio cabin behind the main house (A to G, 12/29/81, 1/1/82, 5/17/83). As often as he can, he travels to the locales memorialized in his fiction—the Yellowstone area, Bryce National Park, the Grand Canyon, the Tonto Rim, Robber's Roost, and especially Brown's Park, his favorite Western "legend spot." He also knows Old Mexico well. He has, however, never been abroad; nor, evidently, does he have any desire "to see the world beyond the West" (A to G, 4/6/82).

Allen habitually indulges in vicarious travel; that is, he reads widely and deeply in Western American history, notably where it relates to American Indians. His favorite authors and books on such subjects are the following, among many others: Eve Ball, John G. Bourke (*On the Border with Crook*), John Rolfe Burroughs (*Where the West Stayed Young*), Thomas J. Dimsdale (*Vigilantes of Montana*), J. Frank Dobie, Josiah Gregg (*Commerce of the Prairies*), George Bird Grinnell, J. Evetts Haley (*Charles Goodnight*), James D. Horan, Meriwether Lewis and William Clark (*Expedition*), Joseph G. McCoy (*Historic Sketches of the Cattle Trade of the West and Southwest*), Martin F. Schmitt and Dee Brown (*Fighting In-*

dians of the West), Stanley Vestal, Walter Prescott Webb (*The Texas Rangers*), and Paul I. Wellman.[14]

Allen also enjoys reading classical and popular literature. He once listed his fifteen favorite authors; they are Edgar Rice Burroughs, Charles Dickens, Sir Arthur Conan Doyle, Sir Henry Rider Haggard, Omar Khayyam, Rudyard Kipling, Jack London, Herman Melville, Sax Rohmer, Rafael Sabatini, William Shakespeare, John Steinbeck, Robert Louis Stevenson, Mark Twain, and H. G. Wells (A to G, 7/13/81). Like his father before him, Allen has an eclectic reading taste. It is curious that Allen until he had written about twenty Westerns of his own never read any by other authors, and further that his bibliophile father never—to Allen's knowledge—read any of his wayward son's literary efforts.[15]

Allen is a popular member of the Western Writers of America. A WWA poll to select the twenty-five best Westerns of all time includes *From Where the Sun Now Stands*, with *I, Tom Horn* one of five runners-up.[16] Among other commendations, he has won five WWA Spur Awards: for the best historical novel of 1960, *From Where the Sun Now Stands*, which also won the 1961 WWA Saddleman (the first, as well as the only Saddleman ever awarded by a vote of the membership); best short story of 1962, "Isley's Stranger"; best historical novel of 1963, *The Gates of the Mountains*; best short story of 1965, "The Tallest Indian in Toltepec"; and best historical novel of 1972, *Chiricahua*, which also won the 1972 Western Heritage Wrangler Award. In addition, Allen received WWA commendations for his 1967 novels *Alias Butch Cassidy* and *One More River to Cross*, and also earned the Outstanding Service Award, National Cowboy Hall of Fame, in 1970.

Allen concludes from reprint data and other sources that the following have been his ten top best sellers: *No Survivors, The Tall Men, The Blue Mustang, Red Blizzard, Mackenna's Gold, The Gates of the Mountains, I, Tom Horn, From Where the Sun Now Stands, Yellowstone Kelly*, and *Santa Fe Passage*. His dozen personal favorites, however, are *No Survivors, The Fourth Horseman, Reckoning at Yankee Flat, From Where the Sun Now Stands, Mackenna's Gold, Chiricahua, One More River to Cross, I, Tom Horn, The Last Warpath, Death of a Legend* (retitled *The Raiders* against Allen's better judgment), *Journey to Shiloh*, and *Maheo's Children* (retitled *The Squaw Killers*, to its advantage—A to G, 10/18/80, 7/11/81).

Sixteen of Allen's novels (including an unpublished science-fiction thriller, *The Day the Sun Died*) have been sold to the movies.[17] Eight have been produced thus far: *The Tall Men* (1955; co-scripted by Sydney Boehm and Frank S. Nugent; directed by Raoul Walsh, music by Victor Young; with Clark Gable, Emile Meyer, Cameron Mitchell, Chuck Roberson, Jane Russell, Robert Ryan, and Will Wright).[18] *Santa Fe Passage* (1955; co-scripted by Lillie Hayward; directed by William Witney; with Rod Cameron, Leo Gordon, John Payne, and Slim Pickens). *Pillars of the Sky* (1956 [*The Tomahawk and the Cross*, British title]; directed by George Marshall; with Michael Ansara, Ward Bond, Jeff Chandler, Frank De Kova, Dorothy Malone, and Lee Marvin). *Yellowstone Kelly* (1959; scripted by Burt Kennedy; directed by Gordon Douglas; with Claude Akins, Warren Oates, and Clint Walker).[19] *Journey to Shiloh* (1968; directed by William Hale; with James Caan and John Doucette).[20] *Mackenna's Gold* (1968; scripted and co-produced by Carl Foreman; co-produced by Dmitri Tiomkin; directed by J. Lee Thompson; photographed by Joe MacDonald; with Lee J. Cobb, Victor Jory, Raymond Massey, Gregory Peck, Edward G. Robinson, Omar Sharif, Telly Savalas, and Eli Wallach).[21] *Who Rides with Wyatt* (1970 [*Young Billy Young*, title]; scripted and directed by Burt Kennedy; with Rodolfo Acosta, John Anderson, Angie Dickinson, Paul Fix, and Robert Mitchum).[22] And *I, Tom Horn* (1980 [*Tom Horn*, title] directed by William Wiard; scripted by Thomas McGuane and Bud Schrake; with Steve McQueen and Linda Evans).[23]

Nineteen of Allen's novels (thirteen Henrys, six Fishers) and two works containing short stories by Allen (as Henry) have been re-issued by British publishers. Thirty of his novels (fourteen Henrys, including two juveniles; sixteen Fishers, including two juveniles) and two works with short stories by Allen (one as Henry, one Fisher) have been translated into foreign languages—often with a single title going into three or four different tongues. Germany has proved the most receptive (nineteen works translated), followed by France (ten), Sweden (nine), and Italy (eight), with Spain (two) and Czechoslovakia (one) bringing up the rear. The fact that Continental readers prefer Allen's Fishers to his Henrys would seem to indicate that they like simpler and more melodramatic action, and less history—although, as previously noted, there is little difference between a typical Henry and a good Fisher. Occasionally, non-American publications of Allen appear under new titles; for example, *The Blue Mustang* becomes *Starbuck*, and *The North Star, Smoke* (A to G, 7/30/81).

Eagle's-Eye View

Because of his fecund versatility, it is hard to organize any comprehensive discussion of Allen's literary works. He has written eighteen novels directly concerned with commercial and military clashes between whites and Indians—mostly Indians of the High Plains, but also including those of the Northwest and Apacheria. Several other Allen novels, not mainly about such conflicts, also include Indian activity. Much of this fiction becomes almost saga-like through the frequent reappearance of key historical figures, such as General George Armstrong Custer, Black Kettle, Crazy Horse, and Sitting Bull, as well as a few fictional characters. In fully thirty-five of Allen's novels Indians figure centrally or tangentially.

A major category of fiction by Allen concerns heroic white and a few Indian horsemen—on the commercial trail to Santa Fe, seeking to raise or raid horse herds, galloping for dear life, punching cattle. Allen is adept at combining history, legend, and fact to retell the saga of such enigmatic figures as Henry Plummer, Wyatt Earp, Butch Cassidy, and Tom Horn. His approach here is a little like that of Emily Dickinson, of all people: to slant the truth, to aggrandize the small, to diminish the great.

Allen has tried his novelistic hand in still other categories. He has written four novels in which war figures importantly. Three concern the Civil War; one, the Spanish-American War. And, fascinated since his youth by tales of lost gold mines, he has published three novels dealing with such legends (one in a contemporary setting); in addition, he wrote one featuring action during the Klondike rush.

He has also written several dozen splendid short stories, all concerning the West, and five books nominally for juvenile readers but, like some of Mark Twain's efforts, grand adult reading as well. Finally, this versatile author has written a novel in a contemporary setting and concerned with escaped convicts, and also two futuristic science-fiction thrillers (one sold to the movies but unpublished and not yet filmed). It would be remiss of me not to add that Allen has done a bit of editing and has written a few minor but informative critical pieces.

Yes, Henry Wilson Allen, alias Will Henry and Clay Fisher, has been productive. Now we ought to see just how productive. Hopo! Hookahey! Let's go. Let's light out after him.

Chapter Two

Indians in Red Cloud's Country and South

Like Francis Parkman before him, Allen has had "Injuns on the brain" from his earliest years. One of his major clusters of novels therefore concerns General Custer, Black Kettle, Sitting Bull, Crazy Horse, Gall, and also various commanders of American military units both before the Little Big Horn and somewhat afterwards. Other Indians such as Dull Knife, Little Wolf, He Dog, and Two Moons, figuring tangentially in Allen's "Custer novels," become central in other Allen fiction. So it is impossible to treat his work in non-chronological groups without some distortion. But, to paraphrase Henry James, one cannot tell the whole of anything, only what hangs together. What hangs together effectively here are five novels by Allen that deal importantly with the background, foreground, and aftermath of Custer's death. They are *No Survivors, Red Blizzard, Yellow Hair, Yellowstone Kelly*, and *Custer's Last Stand*.

Five other novels, forming another but looser unit, concern Indian-white clashes earlier than and just after the battle of the Little Big Horn, and in regions generally south. They are *Warbonnet, The Brass Command, The Pitchfork Patrol, The Squaw Killer*, and *The Day Fort Larking Fell*.

But first the Custer novels.

Custer

No Survivors (1950). *No Survivors* is Allen's first novel and remains one of his best. Brilliantly combining history and fiction, it purports to be the journal of ex-Confederate Colonel John Buell Clayton, who after Appomattox becomes an army scout along the Bozeman Trail. During the massacre of Lieutenant Colonel William J.

Fetterman's command (December 21, 1866) outside Fort Phil Kearny, Clayton is grievously wounded but, rescued by Crazy Horse from among the fallen for his bravery in the fight, is nursed back to health and subsequently adopted "as a son" by Crazy Horse. Clayton is given the name of Cetan Mani (Walking Hawk) and lives for almost a decade in the sacred Black Hills as a Sioux warrior. Turning remorseful after spying on General George "Three Stars" Crook's troop movements before the Battle of the Rosebud (June 17, 1876), he escapes from his Sioux brethren, makes his way to Custer, who he knows from Indian scout reports is in grave danger. The headstrong boy general does not believe Clayton, but Clayton convinces his subordinate Major Marcus A. Reno of the danger and Reno is thus able to save his troops once the military debacle of the Little Big Horn commences.

Now credible fiction turns into captivating fantasy. After Captain Benteen comes to Reno's aid, Clayton joins Captain Weir in seeking to rescue Custer, now doomed. Clayton is severely wounded and goes into cataleptic shock. Thought dead, his body is prepared by his "father" Crazy Horse for ceremonial cremation. Here fantasy yields to something close to allegory. Cetan Mani, escaping under the pyre's smoke on his horse Hussein, finds his wife Star of the North dying in labor to give him a son (later the hero of *The North Star*), hovers unseen when Crazy Horse is bayoneted to death at Fort Robinson (September 5, 1877), kills the war chief's murderer, and makes his way to Sitting Bull, safe at last in Canada. But Sitting Bull tells Clayton that Cetan Mani is dead and must stay that way. So the legendary warrior Walking Hawk pushes on in a sequence reminiscent of the ending of Edgar Allan Poe's *Arthur Gordon Pym* toward Slave Lake, south of which his skeleton is found in the spring of 1878, along with his carefully wrapped journal.[1]

No Survivors is a remarkable first novel. Allen makes Crazy Horse (Tashunka Witko) into an epic figure and Sitting Bull (Totanka Yotanka) into a visionary sage. The heroine North Star is a lovely embodiment of pagan beauty: light of balance like a butterfly, supple as a cat, tigerish, coppery of skin but with a "peach-blow bloom" of sheer radiance.[2] She is Clayton's wound-induced delirium incarnate.

Red Cloud's country is well painted:

A heavy bank of purple cloud hung on the rim of the prairie to the west and as the sun settled into this cover every visible object became coruscated with deep crimson jeweling. The endless prairie snows, gleaming white a moment before, now were stained with scarlet from horizon to horizon. The shouldering hulks of the hills, black and bulky under the dense pine growth, softened into diffused walls of maroon and magenta, flashing here and there a hard battlement of crimson where the naked granite, armored in snow and ice, speared up out of the darker buttresses of the forest. (73)

Allen makes plain where Clayton's sympathies lie, when he has his hero record the following in his journal:

I cursed an endless chain of Army stupidity, white greed, race pride and prejudice. There was no justice in this crazy hatred of Indians. No logic in a great nation hurling armed forces against a people who never at any time could put more than a couple of thousand troops in the field. Oh, yes, there was some logic. Power logic. White logic. These men were red. They ate with their fingers. They called God Wakan Tanka, and worshipped animals. They were heathen. Alien. Dark. Inferior. (57)

By depicting Custer as a blundering glory-seeker, Allen is squarely in the post-1920s tradition. Debunking the boy general had become a popular literary target practice. The first resonant salvo was Frederic F. Van de Water's *Glory-Hunter: A Life of General Custer* (1934). It triggered other anti-Custer accounts, many in novels. The best among scores of those featuring Custer are Ernest Haycox's *Bugles in the Afternoon* (1944), Allen's *No Survivors* (1950), and Thomas Berger's *Little Big Man* (1964).[3] Because his account directed its fire to the consensus-ambushing of the long-haired commander of the Seventh U.S. Cavalry, one might think that Allen must have read widely in Custer fiction. But such was certainly not the case: his sources were not literary at all but historical, especially George Bird Grinnell's *The Fighting Cheyennes* (1915), Paul I. Wellman's *Death on the Prairie* (1934), Stanley Vestal's *Warpath and Council Fire* (1948), and *Fighting Indians of the West* by Martin Schmitt and Dee Brown (also 1948).

The most notable pseudohistorical feature of Allen's *No Survivors* is his occasionally annotating his own hero's journal. For example, just before Custer's death Clayton sees "a captain, unknown to me"

(227). Allen notes that he was Custer's brother Tom. Later Allen also praises the accuracy of Clayton's map of the fatal battlefield.[4]

No Survivors is valuable both as an introduction to Allen and as the source of much work yet to come. It led directly to both his *Yellow Hair* (which led to *The Last Warpath*, which led to *Custer's Last Stand*) and his *Custer's Last Stand*. Meanwhile, what followed was both *Red Blizzard* (which also led to *Custer's Last Stand*) and *Warbonnet* (which led to *The Last Warpath* and *Red Brother and White*).

Red Blizzard (1951).   This novel retells the historical story of the Fetterman massacre, and John "Portugee" Phillips's legendary ride thereafter from Fort Phil Kearny to Fort Laramie, 230 miles, on one horse, and in the −50° dead of winter, to request relief during the subsequent attack by two thousand combined Sioux, Cheyenne, and Arapaho. All of the non-Indian characters have fictional names, and some of the real-life Indians are made to perform fictional deeds. Thus, the hero, based on Portugee, is called Pawnee Perez and is a Sioux-reared Basque-Pawnee half-blood hopelessly ambitious to behave well enough to be accepted as a white man. Colonel Carrington becomes Colonel Travis Clanton, who invades the Powder River territory to build a treaty-breaking fort—to be called not Fort Phil Kearny but Fort Will Farney. Cocksure Colonel W. J. Fetterman becomes Indian-disdaining Major Phil Stacey, subsequently baited and slaughtered by the Indian host at Massacre Hill, on Lodge Trail Ridge, outside Fort Kearny.

Allen reverses the love roles of *No Survivors* by having the half-blood Perez ruinously enamored of Clanton's amorally sexual daughter Lura; and, again, we see Allen's fascination with the romantics of interraciality, which persistently crops up in his work. *Red Blizzard* has too many such verbal and plot echoes from *No Survivors*. It also contains an inordinate amount of scatological verbosity, some of it Rabelaisian in its gusto.[5] But the doom (symbolic in purpose) of the brave half-blood scout, frost-crippled for life by his heroic ride, rejected at its end by faithless white Lura, finally executed as a traitor to his Indian blood by Dull Knife's gory lieutenant Little Wolf, still qualifies this uneven novel as vintage Allen.

Yellow Hair (1953).   Ever intrigued by Custer, Allen soon decided to turn the clock back from the Little Big Horn to the Washita. The result was *Yellow Hair*, in which Custer appears in

fifteen of the twenty-seven chapters and, indeed, provides the title.
Aware of and admiring the boy general's courage in *No Survivors*,
Allen destroys him here. Our first picture of him in *Yellow Hair* is
from the point of view of his friend and scout, Joshua Kelso, at their
reunion:

> Maybe his hair was a mite longer and not so yellow. Maybe his forehead
> had gained another inch in pushing back the skirmish line of his scalp
> against his famous curls. Maybe, too, his jug-handle ears stuck out more
> than ever and his needle-long nose twisted itself more and more to the
> left. But his twitching, woman-small mouth still hid under a sunbleached
> droop of haystack mustache and the little ambush of beard on his chin
> still did its damndest to make him look like he wasn't weak-jawed as a
> pocket gopher. Top all that with the fact that his varmint-close eyes were
> as wild and coyote-looking as ever, and a man had a fair idea of the way
> the "Boy General" sat that present morning of November 13, 1868.[6]

Next we read Joshua's dreadful thought: "Trust Custer. He didn't
mean it to be that way but he could lie himself off any spot you
could corner him on and swear over signature he'd trapped you
there!" (19).

The first essential action is Custer's acceptance of Kelso's idea
for a surprise winter campaign against the hostiles—a strategically
important notion, for which Custer later and ungratefully claims full
credit. Hence scout Kelso does not figure in Custer's memoirs, *My
Life on the Plains*, chapter 10 of which is "The Battle of the Washita."
Kelso, for his part, regards Custer as branded by the devil, but follows
him. Custer chills the scout by concluding at one point: " 'Right now,
killing Indians *is* my business!' " (67). To make "Yellow Hair" even
less attractive. Allen brings in the unpleasant matter of the general's
sexual liaison with Monaseetah, Black Kettle's niece and nominal
interpreter.[7]

The author makes the novel more than cruel history as it marches
toward the well-described Washita battle, by having Joshua also fall
in love with Monaseetah, called by the scout Emoonesta (Bright
Hair). Further, Joshua—like Clayton and Perez before him—has a
divided personality: he hates the army and yet scouts for it, admires
good Indians and yet marches with Custer against them, willingly
kills bad Indians and yet is ashamed of his name among the red men
(Ota Kte, Plenty Kills). Custer is not far from the truth when he

charges Joshua Kelso thus: " 'You keep looking for something decent, noble and chivalrous in them [the Indians], even as you jab half-heartedly at their buffalo-hide windmills' " (63).

Yellowstone Kelly (1957).   The historical background of the superb novel *Yellowstone Kelly* is slighter than it is in *No Survivors*, *Red Blizzard*, or *Yellow Hair*. Allen makes use of only two chapters from the heroic real-life scout's spectacular fourteen-chapter autobiography, published in 1926. In those two chapters Kelly tells about hunting in Montana's Judith Basin and campaigning with General Nelson A. Miles. In chapter 8 Kelly, fresh from Fort Berthold and Fort Buford, recounts his wolf-hunting with a white party, and their entertaining friendly Crow visitors and avoiding unfriendly Sioux warriors. Allen has his Kelly join four neophyte wolfers and survive brushes with a band of Sioux under the real Gall and the fictional Red Paint; Berthold and Buford are both mentioned. In real life Kelly and his associates sold their wolf pelts; in the novel Gall burns the white men's $3,000 haul. Then in his chapter 9 Kelly tells how he sent a huge bear paw to Miles as a "calling card," talked with him about unmapped country beyond the Yellowstone, became his scout, parleyed with Gall, and participated in a December 1876 raid ending in temporary peace. In the novel Kelly does all of these things, but with Gall's and Sitting Bull's activities in December 1876 considerably fictionalized—involved as they must be with Yellowstone Kelly's obligation to return a favor to Gall for his adopting Kelly's injured former mistress Crow Girl, whose son the hero thought was his.

The connection with Custer in this fiction is Kelly's eavesdropping on Sioux plans for the Greasy Grass massacre, galloping for most of six days to warn General Alfred Howe Terry, but arriving a day late. Kelly then unsuccessfully trails Gall for sixty-one days before Miles summons him to become his scout. According to white-man's history— ever suspect to Allen—Kelly got news from the Little Big Horn as it gradually "dribbled in";[8] further, a fellow trapper named John Stanwix took personal delight, says Kelly, in the tragedy because the Indians would thereafter abandon choice hunting grounds in fear of army retaliation. Allen's Kelly, on the other hand, is so in love with Crow Girl that he contemplates converting to Indian ways. The real Kelly relates an anecdote of Stanwix's seeing an Indian's shattered knee treated with hot elk paunch and then operating on the erupting bone fragments. Allen's Kelly himself operates on Crow Girl's bullet-smashed knee; when infection later worsens, the girl asks him to apply an elk-stomach poultice, which works.

It is best to read *Yellowstone Kelly* as fiction. In it we find a little of everything to please almost any palate, and in this order: Eastern greenhorns, poetry-spouting Western hero, descriptions of matchless scenery, honorable and villainous Sioux, phenomenal marksmanship, miscegenated true love (well, almost true), blizzards, pagan honeymooning in a snowbound cabin, evasion of pursuit, fine horsemanship, abduction, manslaughter, quarry circling in Yellowstone National Park, *hinmangas* knife dueling (i.e., castration for the loser), and Montana military movements at −66°. The aesthetic balance of the novel is admirable. Action starts in the Judith Basin, moves to the Yellowstone region, then northeast up the Tongue River. All of this from late 1875 to mid-December 1876. Its five-book structure adds to the novel's unity and conveys a sense of dramatic Indian tragedy. Kelly may be the hero, but then so may Gall be.

Allen recommends *Yellowstone Kelly*, calling it "a lively . . . true story of . . . a classic Irishman and a true humanitarian, not always an easy combination. He [Kelly] may have been the first white non-racist on the frontier who managed it without becoming a squawman. Extremely interesting man" (A to G, 6/4/80). In his preface Allen laments that "[s]oon even the legend [of Kelly] will be lost. The careless winds of time cover deep with history's cynical dust a hundred such obscure heroes and unsung stories of our western past."[9] Allen's novel sweeps such dust from Luther Sage Kelly's name.

Custer's Last Stand (1966). *Custer's Last Stand* represents Allen's last reworking of the Custer story, this time from the Indian point of view. It is in five simple, coherent parts, as was *Yellowstone Kelly*; further, both books flow chronologically. Four of the five parts of *Custer's Last Stand* echo earlier Allen material, thus: Part One—"The Washita"—retells the battle of the Washita, which climaxed *Yellow Hair*. Part Two—"The Pa Sapa [The Black Hills]"—is mostly new, explaining Custer's ruinous reporting of gold in land sacred to the Sioux, but partly old, too, because the Pa Sapa was the locale of Cetan Mani's life with the Sioux in *No Survivors*. Part Three—"Powder River"—freshly tells about Crook's getting the Western command while Custer lolls in New York City and then goes to Washington, D.C., to make an enemy for himself out of President U. S. Grant; Crook meanwhile orders inept Colonel Joseph J. Reynolds to go get Crazy Horse, but he attacks the wrong village. Part Four—"The Rosebud"—repeats details of Crook's defeat as reported in *No Survivors*, which defeat triggered Cetan Mani's return, as Clayton, to the endangered army. And Part Five—"The Little Big Horn"—recounts the story of Custer's defeat and death, then carries the narrative forward to the capture of Crazy Horse, which event provides a post-Custer climax for *No Survivors*.

Custer's Last Stand is distinguished by its straightforward motion and detail. But its most memorable passage comes when Custer, feeling his years now, tells his brother Tom in Hemingwayesque rhetoric how much he admires the enemy: " 'I mean . . . that I think the wild Indian of the American plains has led the finest and noblest life of any man in history. He drinks the cold wind, he is wrapped in the warm sun. He is brave, loyal, generous. He lacks nothing that I admire, or would not give my all, in another life, to share with him.' "[10]

A Miscellany

The next group of five Indian novels to be discussed form a miscellany unified by little more than general geographical place. The locale of *Warbonnet* is between Fort Laramie and Fort Bridger, along the Oregon Trail in Wyoming. *The Brass Command* describes the tragic retreat of Dull Knife to and then out of Fort Robinson in Nebraska. *The Pitchfork Patrol*, largely fiction, occurs out of Fort Pitchfork, Wyoming. *The Squaw Killers* presents action by real and fictional characters against the backdrop of the Sand Creek massacre; *The Day Fort Larking Fell* follows up that tragedy with unique dark-comic action at a fictitious fort based on Fort Larned in Kansas. *The Brass Command, The Squaw Killers*, and *The Day Fort Larking Fell* should generate intense sympathy for abused and lied-to Indians. *The Pitchfork Patrol* features mainly good whites opposing largely honorable Indians, with considerable gore flowing from both sides. Only in *Warbonnet* are the Indians melodramatically treacherous, and even that novel also has a white villain.

Warbonnet (1953).   Like few of Allen's other Indian novels, *Warbonnet* takes place in pre-Civil War times. Its historical *donnée* is the ugly rumor that during the winter of 1853-54 Mormon Brigham Young, who assuredly disliked Jim Bridger, his commercial rival and personal enemy, competed against him by hiring an Arapaho mercenary named Watonga (Black Coyote) to help out. This unpleasant possibility, however, is only secondary to Allen's preposterous plot involving Jesse Callahan, hero of the novel. Callahan is a Minnicon-jou-raised white Bridger scout who opposes murderous Arapahoes attacking his employer's wagons as they move west out of Fort Laramie. Black Coyote has two formidable aides. His barren squaw Ousta (Limper, also called Elk Woman) would like to kidnap the feisty little son of a discouraged white widow named Lacey heading back east with a homesick immigrant party. By professing to nurse Lacey's sick daughter, Ousta gains access to the white group and thus can spy for Watonga. The Indian mercenary also gets help from Tim O'Mara, nominally the leader of the whites but really a renegade Mormon spying for the Arapahoes against Bridger. After her husband had died in the settlements, Lacey married gross Tim to provide a stepfather for her children; but now, regretting the sordid move, she fastens upon Jesse, oddly nine years her junior, as a new and better savior.

A sequence of melodramatic events, including infiltration, captivity, escape, torture, hand-to-hand dueling, and ingenious use of gunpowder by the barrel, provides thrilling reading but not much else. Memorable are Jesse's devotion to Lacey's son and his pursuit of the lad's tooth-some mother, who is frankly—to quote red-headed Jesse—"prime beaver."[11] The curious narrative style of *Warbonnet* resembles that of a loquacious old-timer—talky, folksy, sage, with much animal imagery and Indian lingo—and mitigates what might otherwise be both an improbable and an unacceptably violent plot. For example, the narrator informs us that "[t]here was one stock of goods God never ran himself low on, and that was fools" (33), and that a timely explosion of gunpowder provides "[c]hoice cuts of Chouteau & Company mule, Indian pony and male Arapaho, mingled with a fine selection of oak spokes, hickory whiffletrees and draw-iron wheel rims"—and all with a noise "fit to split a man's earskins clean across" (146).

Allen's "Historical Foreword" says that, while it is a fact that Brigham Young waged "this undeclared, emigrant-business war" with Jim Bridger, it is only "western legend" that Young hired Indian mercenaries. The note closes with a compliment to Mormons in general for their "accepted, heroic part . . . in the settlement of the West" (v). When asked to cite chapter and verse for all of this, Allen replied: "I can't give you a source for the partial anti-Mormon foreword (complete with closing cop-out) in *Warbonnet*" (A to G, 2/20/81).

The Brass Command (1956).   This excellent novel concerns, as does Mari Sandoz's earlier *Cheyenne Autumn*, 1953, the epic journey of the Cheyennes under Dull Knife and Little Wolf from Oklahoma to their homeland in 1878. Being tougher, Little Wolf decides to break off beyond the North Platte River and head for home—Wyoming. Dull Knife, gentler and less militant, proceeds peacefully to Fort Robinson, Nebraska, surrenders to Third Cavalry Captain J. B. Johnson, but is mistreated and starved, then erupts with his forces and their pitiful families in a desperate winter escape— with bloody consequences well known to readers of Western history.

Much is fictional in *The Brass Command*. Allen provides real-life commanding officer Captain H. W. Wessels, who was nominally responsible for the atrocities committed against Dull Knife both at and west of the fort, with the new name of Howell K. "Hollie" Weston, and promotes him to major. Weston is a Civil War hero, a fine cartographer, a friend of General George Crook and his literary adjutant, Captain John G. Bourke, and so long a desk officer that he welcomes the current disastrous Dull Knife affair as a chance to prove something to both the army and himself. What he learns is that he is too humane to succeed militarily in the gory West.

Fictional, too, is the homesteading family of Dutch and Amy Lohburg in dangerous southwestern Nebraska. The ragged tide of Cheyennes rolling north sweeps Dutch Lohburg to his death. The Lohburgs' son Billy is kidnapped, and his widowed mother Amy and his three sisters must flee to Fort Robinson, where Major Weston's magnificent sergeant, John Henry Lundy by name, 6' 6" tall and part Oklahoma Cherokee, decently behaves like the husband and father he will surely become for them. The novel's finest character, brave Little Red Bird, Dull Knife's young grandson, is, like much in Allen's writings on Indians, the result of brilliant fictionalizing on the basis of "material furnished by surviving tribal historians."[12] Red Bird sprang at Allen from a single page in Grinnell's *Fighting Cheyennes*[13] and is made by the inventive novelist to rescue not only little Billy Lohburg but even white-haired Weston himself at one point.

The most horrible scenes in *The Brass Command* present the breakout by Dull Knife's people from the fetid Fort Robinson barracks in which they are cruelly confined, and then the relentless mopping up in the crimson snow afterwards. The most poignant scene offers the reader the response of three imprisoned Cheyenne chiefs when Weston is relieved of command and his remorseless successor, Captain J. T. Jackson (based on J. B. Johnson), takes charge. Warriors Left Hand, Lone Crow, and Wild Hog[14] generously agree that Weston " 'never lied to us' " and shout farewell to the enigmatic major: " *'Enitoeme,* Evoxpohess!' "—which means "We salute you, White Hair!" (151). Perhaps the most memorable speech in the novel comes when the army surgeon checks the corpse of a day-old baby abandoned during Dull Knife's nightmarish retreat over the bitter snow: " 'Born yesterday, froze to death last night, and his mother still on her feet and running. God! The vitality of those women' " (135).[15]

Major Weston is schizoid: brave but vacillating, critical but vapid, indifferent to his orders but meriting his general's respect, humane and religious even while ordering artillery fire on half-frozen Cheyenne families. Is he not the epitome of the American army in the Old West? Split into fascinating counterpoint too is the first half of the novel, as its scenes shift cinematically from the white man's Fort Robinson to the red man's trek north from Oklahoma to Fort Robinson. In chapter 13, which falls at midpoint of the novel, all the principals assemble at the fort for the first time. Then the last half of the novel replicates those very circumstances that drove the Cheyennes to flee from Fort Reno in Oklahoma at the outset, that is, repeated acts of white dishonor.

The Pitchfork Patrol (1962).   Allen insists in another prefatory historical note that the main events of this grade-B melodrama are based on fact: a real patrol under a real cavalry scout, in Wyoming, in August 1877, ordered to rescue a sexy widow and her children. But not out of a fort named Pitchfork; nor was the widow's real name Dulcie Shuffman. Allen excitingly concludes his preface: "Yet little else has been shrouded in this telling of an old Wyoming tale. Its people lived. They did these things, and died or disappeared. What does it matter how they spelled their names?"[16]

Sergeant Honus Schlonager, about forty-five years old, graying, 6' 6" tall and 275 pounds, commands a sea-of-grass ship of fools, a veritable *Pequod* crew of military misfits. They are: a dirty but brave

Sicilian knifer, a British ex-lieutenant and coward from old Khyber Pass days, a criminal Texas ex-cowboy, a Pittsburgh ex-miner wife-killer, an anti-black ex-guerrilla Missouri killer, and a soldier bent on avenging that murderer's slaughter of his brothers.

The theme of this novel is regeneration through violence; so insistently so, in fact, that the patrol's rescue of the Shuffman family seems to be only a metaphor in the fiction's larger argument. The plot is intricate and features feigned death and sudden murder, prairie burials, moronic loyalty, Indian honor, escape by hidden tunnel, severing a hand (with symbolic overtones), dressing a woman in a dead man's uniform, sacrificial suicide, a lickety-split gallop to safety, and—? What finally happened to old Schlonager? Allen is as enigmatic regarding his hero as he habitually is with himself when he concludes that "Schlonager had the Midas touch for being remembered; he knew when to disappear" (164).

The readers of *The Pitchfork Patrol* remember its tangled plot, its extra pint of violence—I counted seventeen corpses (precisely the same as in *Huckleberry Finn*)—the heroine's admirable feistiness, and authenticity of detail.

The Squaw Killers (1968).   This effective and emotional novel, originally entitled *Maheo's Children* and renamed in 1971, presents the attempts of a fictional preacher named Nehemiah Bleek to care for seven Indian orphans at a mission school on Horse Creek near the Arkansas River, in 1864, against the historical background of Colorado Colonel John M. Chivington and his attack on Black Kettle and White Antelope at their Sand Creek camp.[17] In addition to Chivington, Jim Beckwourth, Robert "Jack" Bent, Major Scott J. Anthony, and a few other real-life white, semi-white, military, and quasi-military characters, mostly depicted with scathing criticism, Allen limns one of his finest Indians—Roman Nose. The action starts when this tough Northern Cheyenne warrior brings his orphaned nephew Red Dust down to Bleek's school. Bleek and Roman Nose debate the merits of pacificism until they are ironically interrupted by Colonel Chivington's invasion of the region. What follows, Allen ingeniously avers, was too humiliating to the whites ever to make the history books: the mad colonel, whom the Indians call Mashane (Sick Mind) is so bellicose that he must be taken hostage on a trek toward friendly Indians near Sand Creek. Bleek is too Christian to let Roman Nose do away with the sadistic colonel; so, after complicated maneuvers in the November snow, Bleek releases him and makes his way with his children to a Cheyenne village at Smoky Hill, near Sand Creek, rests, then rushes on to seek help from real-life pro-Indian Major Edward W. Wynkoop at Fort Larned, Kansas, in reassembling his school there.

At this point the plot strands fray apart; the impatient children try to follow beloved Bleek but get lost, are attacked by remnants of Chivington's detachment, and scatter for a while; meanwhile, Bleek, trying to proceed by stagecoach to Pueblo and cooperative agents, is intercepted at William Bent's famous ranch by Chivington. In fact this monster quarantined the ranch to prevent any warning from getting to his intended Cheyenne victims and prepared to attack. Out of this quarantine Allen makes one of the most dramatic scenes in *The Squaw Killers*: Bleek's stagecoach stops. Another passenger, from Leavenworth, is a loquacious female. One of Bent's Cheyenne women alerts the preacher to the hidden presence of Red Dust and the other children, including a wounded girl. A decent soldier and the heroic old stage driver Dirtyface Watson offer to aid. But Chivington rides in, secures the area like a lunatic SWAT officer out of today's TV, and learns through Beckwourth that Red Dust is redoubtable Roman Nose's nephew. When Bleek produces Wynkoop's order of safe conduct, Chivington tears it up. After Bleek and his juvenile charges escape, Chivington darkly promises multiple hangings, scatters imperious orders about, and heads for historic Sand Creek.[18]

The historomantic finale is vintage Allen: Bleek and Red Dust try to warn Black Kettle and White Antelope, but must fail. Yet at least one of them must see enough to substantiate Indian tradition on the attack. How to do so? Well, Bleek is stunned by a ricocheting rifle bullet and hence put out of the action; Red Dust, being only eleven years old, slithers through all the action, like a dusky recording angel, seeing all: Indian chiefs shot while sitting under American and truce flags, the butchering and scalping of demeaningly demonstrative squaws and their children by white soldiers, and unconscionable looting. Red Dust is saved by George Bent, who is like Jack a half-breed son of William Bent. At the end Bleek recovers, gathers his charges, and heads with them for Kansas to build his school—but first to star in *The Day Fort Larking Fell*.

Two additional elements in *The Squaw Killers* require comment. Huge John Chivington and huge Nehemiah Bleek are equally religious and equally fanatic: the former (touched by Satan) to kill nits which make lice (i.e., Indian children, who grow up to become evil), the latter (touched by God, say the Indians) to pacify. And Allen with consummate skill depicts animals here: the Indian children's lame wolfhound named Lamewolf and Bleek's wagon team, the wheelers being Salome and Sheba, the leaders, Samson ("a giant black Spanish jack") and Delilah ("a diminutive piebald Comanche jenny with one sky-blue and one canary-yellow eye").[19] I wonder if Allen is describing some of the beasts that fell on him back in Colorado (where Bleck lived earlier), rearranged his left foot, and caused him to part company from the cowboy life permanently.

The Day Fort Larking Fell (1969). Mark Twain once noted that Richard Wagner's music is better than it sounds. Allen's novel *The Day Fort Larking Fell* is undoubtedly better than it reads, by me, at least. The novel picks up a year or so after the Sand Creek massacre, with Bleek and his orphaned redskin children now in Kansas (for Fort Larking read Fort Larned, Kansas), wrongly imprisoned by the treacherous post commander, and so frustrated in their search for justice and freedom that all hell breaks loose in their subsequent maniacal but successful fight to escape Fort Larking. Is the hell which breaks loose nothing but comedy of the absurd and comedy of the manic abstract? Is Wagner's music nothing but *sturm und drang* Germanic noise? The answer is no to both questions.

The comedy in *The Day Fort Larking Fell* is outrageously told in sequences reminiscent of Geoffrey Chaucer, John Steinbeck, Heinrich Kley, Walt Disney, and Mel Brooks. Allen defends this novel as "a seriously intended effort to make a tragic point (the utter manipulation, betrayal, and degradation of the red man) through the pathetic crudities of *grand guignol*. It is admittedly a 'tour de force,' " Allen concedes, adding that "if it does not work as such, then it is a failure. But it should not be judged or condemned simply because it *is* theatre of the absurd" (A to G, 7/11/81).

This is all well and good, but I think that most readers are likely to be aroused only by the several sight gags in the book—and aroused but temporarily. Fighting between Indians and whites is with the weapons of molasses and flour. An Indian disappears underground when he wears a deep circle during his hours-long pre-combat dance. A charming Indian boy's secret weapon is the enviable pressure of his inexhaustible bladder. Red Dust's old dog trees soldiers and then snaps

at their longjohn trapdoors. A vicious sergeant is shotgunned in the
rear end and left for dead, but later comes to life as he is being
buried. Etc. In the absence of post-commander Major Alexander
Kindthorpe (read Major Edward Wynkoop?), Captain Julius Caesar
Strinker takes charge; this latter-day Caesar alternately preens before
a three-panel mirror dressed in his Custer uniform and evades combat
by turning transvestite. With two memorable little sets of lines from
this curious novel I will close my discussion of it: " 'Bah! What's a
lie? Only something you get caught telling. If they don't learn anything to the contrary, then no untruth has been stated." And ". . . the
white man's fiery *vehoemap* [whiskey] was the most remarkable
invention since squaws."[20]

The ten novels now discussed form a loose but impressive unit.
They move in time from the early 1850s to the end of the 1870s.
Allen used as a backdrop for *Warbonnet* the Mormon-Bridger feud
along the Oregon Trail beyond Fort Laramie. *The Squaw Killers* and
The Day Fort Larking Fell present the pathetic efforts of a white
preacher to mitigate the suffering of little Indian children at the time
of Chivington's raid on the Cheyennes at Sand Creek and thereafter.
Four Custer novels dramatize action from 1865 to the Little Big
Horn and later. Taken together, *No Survivors, Red Blizzard, Yellow
Hair,* and *Custer's Last Stand* mingle fictional action and the history
of many Indian-War battles: the Fetterman massacre, the siege of
Fort Phil Kearny, the Washita, the Powder River campaign, the
battle of the Rosebud, the destruction of Custer's Seventh Cavalry,
and the breakup of the Sioux under Crazy Horse, Gall, and Sitting
Bull. Allen also wrote *Yellowstone Kelly,* in the background of which
are Custer but in more detail Sitting Bull and Gall after Custer's
death. Further, Allen offered *The Brass Command,* showing that Little
Wolf and Dull Knife, both Cheyennes, were doomed once they and
the Sioux of Sitting Bull and Crazy Horse had their fatal falling
out—Fort Reno, Fort Robinson, and the bloody retreat of January
1879 followed like action in a Greek tragedy. *The Pitchfork Patrol*
may be dated 1877, but its action could easily have occurred a year or
two earlier, or a little later.

Reading the ten novels not only is exciting but also provides a
history lesson of range and depth. Allen admires bravery on both
sides, but his heart is clearly with the once-free and usually noble
High Plains warriors.

Geographically the ten novels spread from what is now Oklahoma (the Washita, Fort Reno) through Kansas (Fort Larned), to Colorado (Sand Creek), to Nebraska (Fort Robinson), and then through Wyoming (Fort Phil Kearny) to southern Montana (the Powder River, the Rosebud, the Little Big Horn). Allen's descriptions of specific locales are often incidental, but the novelist shares both his geographical knowledge and his love of Western regions with all willing readers.

Chapter Three

Indians in the Northwest and Deep Southwest

In addition to Indian novels motivated by Custer, and those dealing with trouble on the Oregon Trail, or east, or along Sand Creek, Allen's canon includes three novels cast along the route of Lewis and Clark, both during their time and later. These are *Pillars of the Sky, From Where the Sun Now Stands*, and *The Gates of the Mountains*. Four other Allen novels centrally concern Apaches a thousand or more miles southeast. These are *The Seven Men at Mimbres Springs, The Apache Kid, Chiricahua*, and *Apache Ransom*.

Categorizing Allen's Indian novels into those concerned with the Northwest and the Deep Southwest is always loose. For example, the time of *The Bear Paw Horses* coincides with that of the last three-fifths of *From Where the Sun Now Stands*, which dramatizes Nez Percé Chief Joseph's 1877 retreat; *The Bear Paw Horses* tells of the attempt of a group of people, Sioux and otherwise, to supply Joseph with horses and thus prevent his surrender. However, discussion of *The Bear Paw Horses* comes later because its action concerns "heroes and horses" more than it does Indians of the Northwest. For another example, the seven men of *The Seven Men of Mimbres Springs* are at the springs because of the Civil War; yet since they go into action against Apaches west of Texas, their story connects with Southwestern Indians. *The Crossing* also includes countless Apaches; however, since its central impulse is the Civil War I take it up later.

The Northwest

Pillars of the Sky (1953).   Obviously seeking a new locale and an unpopularized segment of Western history, Allen after *No Survivors, Red Blizzard*, and *Santa Fe Passage* (yet to be discussed) seized upon the Washington-Idaho region just before the Civil War. The result was *Pillars of the Sky*. (Its original title, *To Follow a Flag*, is more meaningful.) In this novel, his fifth, Allen demonstrates his versatility by introducing the following innovations: a flawed but honest officer (Major Weston of *The Brass Command*, cast in the same mold, would come later), a renegade soldier of unquestioned loyalty and great panache, an all-white love affair (*No Survivors, Red Blizzard*, and *Santa Fe Passage* feature interracial sexuality), and a black female captured by Indians whom she prefers to her former white masters (Allen portrayed more significant blacks later, in *The Seven Men at Mimbres Springs, San Juan Hill, The Gates of the Mountains, One More River to Cross, See How They Run*, etc.). New also is a pro-white Christian Indian scout of great dignity and honor. This tribesman of the Nez Percés is Tamason, christened Timothy, and is thé heroic follower of his adopted flag.

Action begins when Lieutenant Colonel Edson Stedloe starts moving too many soldiers from Fort Wallowa, near Walla Walla, north along the Colville Road toward Washington territory gold fields, to force a peace with Palouse Indian chief Kamiakin. When the colonel swings east into sacred Indian territory, trouble starts. A combination of actions by alcoholic Sergeant Emmett D. "Emm" Bell and by Timothy circumvents Indian retaliation, which includes not only the abduction of Bell's estranged love, Calla Lee Rainsford of Virginia, but also some gory skirmishing. Stedloe alternately arrests and coddles the irrepressible Emm, who snatches Calla from Kamiakin's lodge only to attempt sexual assault once they are back in his tent. He subsequently redeems himself by commendable military assault.

Western historians will recognize that Stedloe owes almost everything to real-life Lieutenant Colonel Edward J. Steptoe of Fort Walla Walla, who in May 1858 provoked Kamiakin north of Fort Lapwai. Though more of a loner, Timothy is based on Chief Timothy, whose Nez Percés helped Steptoe cross the Snake River both going and returning. Of aid to fictional Sergeant Bell is real-life Lawyer, a Nez Percé chief, who spies on Kamiakin's movements. Allen, as he did in *No Survivors* and would do often later, provides a detailed map—in this case one showing the region north and northwest of Walla Walla—based as he notes on the 1858–62 surveys of "Capt. J. Mullins" (really Lieutenant John Mullan).[1]

We must remember that Allen is a novelist, not a historian. *Pillars of the Sky* is an adventure story involving in-depth characterization. Stedloe is strange. He offers the most illogical analysis imaginable of Kamiakin's plot-pivoting attack on a civilian wagon train: the chief could not have known—could his scouts have had time to report?—that the army had moved east in premeditated violation of peace-treaty terms by the time of the wagon burning. In other words: Yes, we acted criminally, but you should not have done likewise because you could hardly have known what we were doing!

Emm Bell is more than strange. Twice at least his conduct is Hawthornean in its unconsciously compulsive motivation. After Calla escapes his nocturnal sexual advances, Emm "through no conscious direction of his own . . . veered to bring up against a small pyramid of darkness, . . . Stedloe's tent,"[2] where Calla is hiding. Later, during the night following the battle, Emm returns almost suicidally to stay with a mortally wounded enlisted man, left behind. Both of these actions parallel elements in "Roger Malvin's Burial."[3]

Calla is most strange. Still loving the man who offered rape, she delivers two of the most moving lines in the whole book. As Sergeant Bell, blind with fatigue in the pitch dark, weaves silently at her tent flap, she senses his proximity and whispers, " 'Who's there, please?' " By the time she peeps out, he is gone and all she can say is, " 'Emm? Oh, Emm, is it you?' " (111). In context, these tiny speeches crackle with emotional voltage.

Timothy is the hero of virtually all the action. He is sustained by faith in his adopted flag and especially in his Choosuklee (Chinook for "Jesus Christ").

From Where the Sun Now Stands (1960).   Timothy in *Pillars of the Sky* recalls that his "father . . . walked with Lewis and Clark these fifty-two winters gone" (102). The end of the long walk with the whites was for the Nez Percés spelled out on October 5, 1877, when Chief Joseph, whose grandfather also was a Lewis and Clark expedition guide, delivered one of the most emotional speeches ever heard on the continent of North America. It ends: "Hear me, my chiefs. I am tired; my heart is sick and sad. From where the sun now stands, I will fight no more forever."[4]

In an acknowledgments page at the end of *From Where the Sun Now Stands* Allen cites eleven historical and linguistic sources, one unpublished, which he used for this prize-winning novel. He also hints that he consulted much else. All of this unusual identification of source material suggests an inordinate desire to be regarded here as devoted to accuracy. Add now the fact that Allen once said, "I think I'll stand or fall with *From Where the Sun Now Stands*," which he feels is "typical of . . . [his] work, and good" (A to G, 4/27/80).[5]

Allen's story of Chief Joseph (Heinmot Tooyalakekt—Thunder Traveling to the Mountain) is like a Gobelin tapestry, with successive panels providing a vivid historical backdrop interwoven with painterly fiction. So much happens as we move from scene to scene that the effect resembles that of Willa Cather's *Death Comes for the Archbishop.*

The narrator of Allen's novel is Heyets (Mountain Sheep). At the outset he is fourteen years old, an undersized, appealingly homely Nez Percé pony-herd boy in the Wallowa. He is also the nephew of Chief Joseph. The Christian religion of his reservation-schooled Indian mother tugs the reluctant lad toward the whites initially. But their rapaciousness and lies, as well as his love of one Indian girl (Meadowlark, later bayoneted to death by white soldiers during a fierce combat scene) and then another (Beaver—she "had lost the two big teeth in front and gained the lovely curves behind" [144]), turns Heyets into a hawk-eyed, killer scout under Joseph during that wizard's 113-day, 1,300-mile retreat from the American army. The Nez Percés move from White Bird Canyon, across the Clearwater River into the Bitterroot Range to Fort Missoula and then to the settlement of Stevensville; next across the Lolo Trail to the Big Hole and Camas Creek, scenes of battle; then to Canyon Creek on the Yellowstone River, Cow Island in the Missouri River, and into the Bear Paw Mountains—scene of surrender, near Canada and freedom.[6]

Allen researched published accounts of the retreat and then has his Indian narrator conclude: "The white history tellers talk with many tongues and they are not all straight" (73). The novelist's intention is to redress the record by presenting his historomance through the Nez Percé eyes of Heyets, who, after explaining at one point his inability to summarize the enemy's deployment of infantry, cavalry, and artillery, laments: "This is the way a white man remembers a battle. . . . But not an Indian. An Indian remembers where his mother fell bayoneted, or his little brother had his skull smashed, or his sister cried for mercy and was shot in the mouth. Still, the one way is history and the other only Indian lies" (175, 176). Red Nose (Colonel John) Gibbon, Bearcoat (Colonel Nelson A.) Miles, Slow Fighter (Colonel Samuel D.) Sturgis, and even One Hand

(General Oliver O.) Howard all come in for scathing criticism here.

By contrast, Heyets gives us a charming depiction of the Indian love of life. The Nez Percés savor each season of the year. Heyets loves spring in May, the camas meadows in June, the root harvest in July, and then August thanksgiving. But he so hates the idea of going to the Lapwai missionary school starting in September that he contemplates intertribal murder to avoid it by thus gaining adult status. He approves of a dream visionary's denunciation of redskin farmers and miners: " 'You ask me to plough the ground. Shall I then take a knife and tear at my mother's bosom? You ask me to dig for stone of gold. Shall I therefore dig under her skin for her bones? You ask me to cut the long grass and make hay to sell and become rich like the white men. But how will I dare cut off my own mother's living hair?' " (44). Opting for the rich, free, old ways, Heyets and his young friends race horses through the wide-open spaces and conclude with Joseph: "The white man knew that to pen up the Indian in a small place was to destroy his spirit, to break his heart, to kill him" (23).

Joseph dominates all others in this epic, is uniquely portrayed and never reduced to a stereotype, is intellectual rather than militant, and concludes that all his options will eventuate in tragedy.[7] He is an advocate of courteous compliance with and passive resistance to the greedy whites, on whom he lectures with withering honesty to his people. We never see him firing at the enemy; instead, he speaks soothingly and in a Christian manner, cautions sagely, protects women and children, never cries over spilled milk, and once even votes with two wrong-headed war chiefs—Toohoolhoolzote (Harsh Sound, of the Salmon River band) and Peopeo Hihhih (White Bird, of the White Bird band)—to show the people unity. Joseph has the power to see the road ahead, the road of time and the road of events. Once, he generalizes in a Melvillean way, though more depressingly, when he avers, " 'Life is a river of sorrow, old friend. You cannot come to it, you cannot cross over it, without knowing some sorrow. You cannot look up the river only to the sunrise; you must look down it toward the darkness, too' " (61).

But Allen dramatizes two victories beyond Joseph's vision of darkness. First, White Bird escapes; he did so in real life, and his doing so enabled Allen to direct the action of another novel, *The Bear Paw Horses*, toward that escape. And second, Heyets also escapes and thus can show anew the veracity of the noblest generalization in *From Where the Sun Now Stands*: it concerns love, "that brief hour which is life's best" (145). Allen says little more about love here, perhaps sensing with Heyets, one of the finest if also the homeliest of his heroes, that the best natural element in the whole fair land of the Nez Percé is—silence. Just before whispering *"Taz alago, taz alago, Aihits Palojami.* Good-bye, good-bye, oh dear Fair Land," Heyets notes that "there was a stillness in that place which made the ears ache" (136, 134).[8]

The Gates of the Mountains (1963).   We know that Allen linked both Timothy, scout in *Pillars of the Sky*, and Chief Joseph, sage of *From Where the Sun Now Stands*, with the Lewis and Clark expedition through their Nez Percé ancestors. Naturally enough, therefore, one might have predicted that Allen would sooner or later bring Meriwether Lewis and William Clark into greater prominence in a subsequent novel. He did—in *The Gates of the Mountains*, a work which achieves a level of excellence hardly exceeded even by *From Where the Sun Now Stands*. Perhaps only the tragedy of Joseph's story makes it more compelling art than *The Gates of the Mountains*, which is a success story.

Here Allen scores a technical coup by having as his central character François Rivet, an exciting, real-life person. He is, however, barely mentioned in the original *Journals*. In the novel young Frank is an eighteen-year-old half-breed son of Achille Rivet and a Pawnee squaw. The father was once a boatman out of St. Louis but was captured long ago, sold to Shoshones in the Northwest, and later called a living dead man in Indian legends. Frank's motivation is as old as that of Joseph Campbell's "hero with a thousand faces"[9]—he wants to join the Lewis and Clark expedition both to have fun and to find his father. Clark, physically tough and more heart than head, is willing to let the lad come along; but Lewis, better educated, more head than heart, and also nominally in command, creates dramatic tension by forbidding him to do so, even though Frank in the first chapter saves Clark's keelboat from smashing up in the wild Missouri River, on May 24, 1804.

So Frank stows away, is befriended by Clark and also Clark's black slave York, and is reluctantly permitted by Lewis to accompany the party both as oarsman and as Clark's secretary. Frank helps later when he hand-talks with three Yankton Sioux past the Niobrara

River, on the Upper Missouri. Later the Teton Sioux let the expedition proceed, in part because young Frank reminds them of his "drowned" father Achille, whom they remember.

Now comes Allen's finest stroke. Mysterious Frank Rivet meets Sacajawea, the most fascinating Indian woman in Western history. When Clark hires Toussaint Charbonneau as interpreter during some construction work in the land of the Mandans, north of the Cannonball River, unreliable Charbonneau's second squaw enters. She is Sacajawea, originally a Shoshone, but kidnapped by the Minnetarees and now here, aged sixteen, pregnant, competent in Indian tongues, and—to young Frank—ravishing. His love for her is Allen's fictional touch; her love for Clark both has historical warrant and is played up by the novelist for its dramatic value. Frank and Sacajawea agree to be brother and sister, and she encourages him by reporting that she knows his father is alive and with the Shoshones.

After a winter (1804–5) of multiple hardships—unfriendly Sioux, rabid wolves, Sacajawea's painful childbearing, with Clark midwifing—the expedition moves on. At Frank's suggestion, Sacajawea goes along since the party needs horses, and the girl's brother, Cameahwait, is the new chief of the distant Shoshones and can help. Sullen spring brings new problems: sickness near Great Falls, the difficulties of a portage, torrential flooding, crippling hail, and geographical confusion at Three Forks. The Forks are more than watery; they are symbolic as well, for it is here that Frank is ordered to leave the party and seek his father.

Allen skillfully conflates Frank's disappointment but concomitant resumption of duty, and a very dramatic moment in the real history of Lewis and Clark (August 17, 1805)—Sacajawea's ecstatic reunion with her brother. He soon provides necessary horses for the explorers; Sacajawea proceeds west with the party as agreed; and Frank, planning to rendezvous with the whites the following June in preparation for their return to St. Louis, goes with the Shoshones to seek his father. In one of the most dramatic scenes in all of Allen's work Frank Rivet is led by sympathetic Indians to his father and sees for himself that because of the old man's near-drowning he is, though still handsome, straight-limbed, and noble in mien, now insane and "mute as the mountain"—but also loved by children, protective of them, and able to whistle "sweetly and poignantly and melodiously and cheerfully as the prairie lark."[10]

The rest of the novel in essence amounts to little more than a debate between Frank's Gallic nature and his Indian nature. He kills an important Minnetaree enemy, reunites with Clark and the other whites, loses a horse herd to marauding Crows, feels alienated from both Clark and York, and begins to view Sacajawea as squaw-like when she boils an ungutted, unskinned dog and dribbles tobacco juice into the pot. Will it be Fort Mandan with the Charbonneau family or St. Louis for Frank? Will he resume the name François Rivet? Will he favor his Indian name—Tooettecone (Black Rifle)? Will he become his father?[11]

More than in any other novel, Allen in *The Gates of the Mountains* relies upon a source. His frontispiece is a map of the exploration route, St. Louis to Fort Clatsop, 1804–6. Action in every one of the fifty-six chapters in the novel may be dated, often to the day. Over and over Allen quotes from the journals of Lewis and of Clark. Almost forty persons named by the explorers figure in Allen's action. Half a hundred place names add to a sense of verisimilitude. But the novelist does not merely fictionalize aspects of an event of unique importance in history. He also rescues an otherwise nearly forgotten fellow named a few times in the historical journals and attendant documents, breathes life into him, then has him meet and love but not get Sacajawea, whom neither Allen nor anyone else needs to rescue from any oblivion ever.[12]

Allen's purpose is not to introduce historical characters, but to present aesthetically pleasing historomance. The novel is brilliantly unified by a pattern of counterpoint. Frank alternately succeeds and fails, joins and is repulsed, brings a search for his father to a successful conclusion but is almost destroyed by what he finds, attaches himself to Clark and to York but ultimately is neither the former's "Pawnee" nor the latter's " 'white boy' " (225, 213). Frank aches for Sacajawea on any terms until he notes at one late point that "Sacajawea's Brother Frank died silently beneath the winking, cold, high stars of Goatpen Creek" (230).

Southwestern Indians

Several of Allen's most action-packed novels are set in Apacheria and in hellish climes nearby, and feature a unique blend of historical personages such as Mangas Coloradas, Al Sieber, Pa-nayo-tishn

("Peaches"), Henry Ossian Flipper, and dread Juh, with fictional heroes and heroines named Linn Sparhawk, Lucille Louise Henderson, Wandermere, Mrs. Carter, Padre Panfilo Alvar Nunez, Ben Allison, and Huera. Often, it seems probable that little fictionalizing is done; I even suspect that supposedly made-up names might be traced to obscure historical sources by readers of ingenuity and patience.

Allen's Apache and Comanche novels may be fewer than those dealing with Sioux, Cheyenne, Nez Percé, Mandan, and Shoshone people; but the half-dozen or so that do concern Southwestern Indians make up in violence for what they lack in numbers. They stress fiction more than history.

The Seven Men at Mimbres Springs (1958). This novel is unusual in many respects. Only in *Santa Fe Passage* (to be discussed later) does Allen treat aspects of Southwestern history earlier in his career. Moreover, *The Seven Men at Mimbres Springs* is his first novel with a Civil War background—that is, if we do not count *The Raiders*, which depicts Jesse James almost entirely after the war. But more important, *The Seven Men at Mimbres Springs* is the first novel in which Allen presents Apaches in their legendary ferocity.

The Seven Men at Mimbres Springs is not a totally successful novel, but it is thoroughly absorbing. The historical background is shadowy and minor. The date is early April 1861. The heroine, named Lucille Louise Henderson—"Lucy," aged nineteen—is a pretty, inexperienced, and scared Union counterspy whose mission is to secure the operational records of the John Waterfield stagecoach line west from El Paso, Texas, to California,[13] in order to prevent the Confederacy from using the plans to establish a route of its own for running California gold into rebel war coffers. The seven men inspiring Allen's title comprise a Chaucerian gallery of types. Little Linn Sparhawk is a pro-Union Alabaman and an employee of the Waterfield Company in El Paso. Doc Harnaday is a gabby, tough old stagecoach driver. Frank L. Swango is a pro-Union gunman, gray-haired but cool. Ceferino "Cipher Reno" Sanchez is a teen-aged half-breed typically anxious, like Pawnee Perez, Timothy, and François Rivet, to cross the color line and become an *Americano*. Jack Berger-man is a German-Jewish migrant to southwest Texas. Ex-slave Simon "Sim" Peter is a gigantic, noble Massai, loyal to Sparhawk, who bought him his freedom. Then there is Price Cullross, a San Antonio

secessionist who winds up with the Union group because of luck—
some good, but a lot bad.

What might have been a routine dash out of El Paso to freedom,
victory, and surely love, becomes something different under Allen's
hand. The seven men and young Lucy suffer from divided leadership,
which results in confused progress to Mesilla, then a timorous pro-
Southern town, past Fort Fillmore, which the group mistakenly concludes is abandoned, then to Membrace Station, near Fort Webster,
and back to Mimbres Springs.

This Edenic little oasis, near which Lucy and Linn have a predictably sexy swim (see No Survivors, Yellow Hair, etc.), becomes the
fatal locale of the last half of the novel. Once the group has outrun
pursuing secessionists, it is surrounded by Apaches. We are prepared
for their chief's appearance by reminiscence flashing from old Harnaday
to young Linn, which reaches back to San Jacinto and Monterrey, then
forward to 1856, Cochise and the "Cherry Cows," Benito, Victorio,
then to 1860 and Apache attacks from Gila Bend to Yuma, and to
the army's foolish attempt to trap Cochise two months before the
novel starts. After the first attack at Mimbres Springs, Harnaday asks
Linn to scan the Apache leader with field glasses and describe him.
Linn obliges: " 'Tall for an Apache, real tall. And big. Thick-bodied
as a bull. Got a head the size of a nail keg. Tough and craggy-faced
but not mean-looking. Appears level-tempered, maybe even friendly.
He's . . . wearing an odd outfit, all right. Regular sort of a suit or
uniform rig of some kind . . .' "[14] Harnaday interrupts to ask whether
the man is wearing a pair of red sleeves. Yes. So he is Mangas Coloradas—the redoubtable Red Sleeves himself, hero of a thousand
tales.[15]

During the rest of the novel Linn, often outvoted in reversals of
formulaic fiction but proved correct, goes serenely about the business
of trying to save Lucy's life at least. We sympathize with the out-
numbered band, as they are picked off one by one. The Apaches are
depicted here as too stupidly patient to merit much respect; in addition, they are vile Mimbreños and even kill one of the seven by
ramming a red-hot rifle barrel into his bowels and beyond.

The novel is marred by a serious weakness but graced by a stunning narrative frame. If the Waterfield mission is crucial to the Union,
then the forces in Washington, D.C., should have sent a better agent
than timid Lucy. But intriguing is her enigmatic fate. Did she dress

as a comely woman, walk safely into Red Sleeves' camp and, under his "cold-eyed empty face" (166), stay with her Indian captors and bear dead Linn's son, survive immemorially long to die about 1950 on a reservation in New Mexico, and leave a diary and other telltale effects? Implying as much and more are Prologue and Epilogue.

The Apache Kid (1961).   Less well known than Mangas Coloradas was the mysterious Apache Kid. This shadowy individual was a renegade after Geronimo's surrender. He had been a scout (with the rank of sergeant, under chief of scouts Al Sieber) for the American army against the Chiricahuas, married a daughter of Chief Eskiminzin, and killed his father's Apache murderer in 1887. Surrendering their weapons at San Carlos, in Arizona territory, the Apache Kid and his subordinate scouts became alarmed at a rumor that they were to be exiled in Florida; gunfire followed, and the Kid fled but soon returned to General Miles for a trial which was rigged to result in a sentence of execution; that was commuted to a term in Alcatraz and then, in 1889, to Yuma. Apache prisoners being transported there overpowered and killed the two guards, leaving the driver wounded. The Kid fired no shots but escaped—into legend. Eskiminzin may have helped his son-in-law remain at large. In 1894 an Arizona miner named Ed Clark shot at and killed a female Apache and wounded her companion close to his cabin. Was the second person, who melted into the darkness, the Apache Kid?

With special cleverness, Allen takes this plot skeleton and fleshes it into *The Apache Kid* (original title: *Niño*), one of his most imaginative stories. We read of the Kid Niño's childhood at Camp Grant and his early scouting work, his surrender and flight, his being befriended by an immaculate friend—his Apache pal Packrat—as well as by Apache scouts Josh and Nosey. Allen provides Niño with two women, first lovely Chuana, Eskiminzin's daughter, and then lumpish Hoosh. Associating with the Kid is fatal to both. Chuana, after bearing Niño's son in their Verde Valley pueblo paradise, dies because of a brush there with a homicidal rival Apache named Logarto (Lizard). Hoosh dies by Clark's gun, aimed at the elusive Kid.

The seventeen-chapter novel has distinct symmetry. In the pivotal middle chapter the Kid leaves his baby with Packrat's old mother, who tries to save it from the army but freezes to death with it. Chuana dies one chapter before the middle one; Hoosh, one chapter before the last one. The Kid has two main friends, Packrat and Al

Sieber. One is dark, the other white. The Kid has two special enemies, dark Lizard and white Clark. Lizard wounds Sieber in the first chapter; Sieber tends the gravely wounded Kid in the last chapter. All through the novel the Kid tries to follow both "civilized" law (with his army-trained head) and tribal law (according to his Apache heart). Similarly, Allen tries to follow both "the hard words of the white man's history" and "the half-century-old Indian tales," to produce "both the lights and the shadows of the legend that was Niño, the Apache Kid."[16]

The plot is exciting but not memorable. What is poignant is Niño's being a man without a country, almost without a tribe; also the devotion shown him by Chuana, Hoosh, and Packrat. The whites generally come off badly here, except for Sieber. The legend lives. So does the scenery of Apacheria, which is starkly painted.

Chiricahua (1972). *Chiricahua* is without doubt Allen's best Apache novel. It has more violent action than *The Seven Men at Mimbres Springs*. It has almost as much Apache lore as *The Apache Kid*. It escorts us into Mexico, as will *Apache Ransom*. And it dramatizes camaraderie and true love much the way *Black Apache* will. *Chiricahua* in addition features an anti-hero, as do many of Allen's works. Here the central character is drifter, horse thief, drunkard, would-be revenge seeker, and robber, curiously without a name until the Epilogue. (Then he is called Wandermere.)

The plot is of undiagrammable complexity, with many lines of action converging on the drifter. An inept army unit operates under a stupid lieutenant ordered to quell the 1883 Chiricahua Apache raids. Peaches is that unit's scout, but he has become separated from it; this real-life hero, named Pa-nayo-tishn (The Coyote Saw Him), was also called Tzoe by his White Mountain Apache family. With less anguish we also follow the tribulations of a stageline owner-operator, an aging sheriff and his disloyal, foul-talkin' deputy, and a pregnant white stagecoach passenger who hopes to get to Fort Lowell, near Tucson. In addition to pro-white Peaches, we have the following anti-white Indians: real-life Chato (Flat Nose), on the trail of Apache vengeance against the army for killing some of his women; Lucero, another murderous Apache and Chato's sexual rival; and a lovely Cheyenne-Crow woman named Estune, who lost her baby to army guns and will do what she must for a replacement.

If the plot of *Chiricahua* is a maze, the unities of place and time are clear: west toward Fort Lowell, south deep into Apacheria, north again to Lowell, then east again and north into Wyoming, no less; and all of this late in March and into April 1883.

Chiricahua is a late Allen novel. In it the author draws on much of his earlier fiction instead of being more inventive with respect to characterization and plot. The army is as ineffective as it was in *No Survivors, Red Blizzard, Pillars of the Sky, The Brass Command,* and *The Apache Kid.* The army unit has a tough sergeant who, precisely as did his predecessor in *The Pitchfork Patrol,* survives to wander west into legend. Loyal Peaches is held in as much suspicion as were native scouts in *Red Blizzard, Pillars of the Sky,* and *The Apache Kid.* Stageline details are repeated from *The Seven Men at Mimbres Springs* and *The Squaw Killers.* The white woman appeals to the hero longer than suits perceptive readers, as is the situation in *Red Blizzard* and *The Crossing* (to be discussed later); further, the drifter's resistance to dark skin may be likened to that of the heroes of *Santa Fe Passage* (to be considered shortly) and *The Crossing.* Chato attacks murderously but often as ineptly as Mangas Coloradas's cohorts did around Mimbres Springs. Beautiful Estune is motivated too much the way barren Elk Woman was in *Warbonnet.* Clooney Borrum is a captivatingly presented black man in *Chiricahua*—loyal, patient, versatile, generous, and enduring—but is reminiscent of York from *The Gates of the Mountains* and much like Isom Dart of *One More River to Cross* (yet to be treated).

In *Chiricahua* Allen provides a parade of violent actors, in gory new combinations. With this violence comes some of the most scatological language since *Red Blizzard*—mostly from the vile tongue of Deputy W. K. "Pinky" Suggins, Jr. The reader will long remember the skillful movement of action from place to place. Each of the novel's ten parts is named for a specific locale, real or fictitious. But the reader will remember even longer, not heroic Peaches or the white drifter, but pantherish, brave, gorgeous Estune. I recommend *Chiricahua* unstintingly as an ideal introduction to Allen's fiction since it is a mile-long film clip of his best special effects.

Apache Ransom (1974). "I sensed the sudden quickening of the fates that ever seems to funnel the affairs of men to a common end from many separate beginnings"[17]—so records Padre Panfilo Alvar Nunez, narrator of Allen's most ingenious fictional concoction, *Apache Ransom.*

As for myself, I sense that in *Apache Ransom* Allen funnels so many different streams of history and fiction that the result almost drowns the reader with information and emotion. To begin with, we are presented with Padre Nunez's manuscript account, discovered only in 1933 in a Catholic sacristy in Ciudad Juarez, near El Paso. Nunez records his fear that Juh, the Apache *jefe*, will return to do him in. But Allen gives us not merely Juh but also the redaction of an 1868–73 yarn about the kidnapping by Apaches of a Texas governor's young son; Buck Buckles, the lad, who speaks English like Huckleberry Finn but Spanish like a little grandee, rather enjoys being held in exchange for guns and ammunition from the Fort Bliss arsenal, and thinks it might even be fun to be half Apache and half Texas *pistolero* in adulthood. Allen weaves Ben Allison into the story, too. By 1974 Ben had already figured in four "Tall Man" novels— *The Tall Men, The Big Pasture, Return of the Tall Man*, and *Outcasts of Canyon Creek* (all to be discussed later). In this latest story Ben has promised young Buck's dying mother, a friend of Ben's own abducted sister, to join the Texas Rangers in pursuit of Juh down into Mexico.

The resulting narrative throws Ben, Nunez, Buck, and Juh together. But the narrative bottle under Allen's fictive funnel has more room. Enter Lieutenant Henry Ossian Flipper, mysterious real-life black West Point graduate.[18] Allen converts him into Robert E. Lee Flicker, former black army sergeant once on duty at Fort Bliss, once scout into Apacheria, now admirer of the Apache way of life. Flicker was victimized when his old West Point roommate and nemesis—now Lieutenant Jefferson Flowers—raped his own fiancée, blamed the innocent black, and got him cashiered. Flowers then followed Flicker to Fort Bliss and framed him again out there. Allen can pour yet more ingredients through the funnel. In addition to assorted Apaches including Kaytennae, Otsai, and Loco, the novel adds plot fluid from two evil vials: (1) Huera, a female Apache of great beauty and ferocity, loves Flicker, seeks to promote him over Juh in the latter's own famed Sierra Madre stronghold, fears the spiritual power of Nunez, and is nursed by kind Ben after she was gang-raped by (2) Santiago Kifer and his white Tejano scalp-hunters, who seek amnesty for crimes north of the border in return for leading Lieutenant Flowers to Juh's stronghold south of the border.[19]

Believe it or not, the direction the tightly spun plot takes is simple. Mostly we follow Ben's line of action as the tall Kwahadi-Texan alternately pursues little Buck's Apache abductors, falls into their clutches, escapes them only to aid them, is caught again, is free again.

Free? Caught? Ben's status changes eight times in the novel.

At the end the reader hopes that durable Ben will figure in still another story. Perhaps he will be able to find his long-lost sister? Flicker and Nunez are still alive though not secure. And vicious Kifer has unfortunately survived. Allen left *Apache Ransom* open-ended enough to permit serial continuation—just as in the Saturday afternoon movies.

The above seven novels, dealing with Indians in the Northwest and in Apacheria, do not constitute all of Allen's Indian stories. *Santa Fe Passage* and *The Blue Mustang* tell of Indian fights but center mainly on white horsemen. Most of the other novels featuring Ben Allison also concern Indians, as do *Reckoning at Yankee Flat*, *One More River to Cross*, *I, Tom Horn*, two of Allen's Civil War novels, and all of his gold-mine yarns, especially *Black Apache*, which is a continuation of *Apache Ransom*. But since these novels mainly fall in other categories of fiction by versatile Henry W. Allen, they will be discussed subsequently and not with his Indian tales.

It may be correct to say that Allen's best fiction presents Indians in a sympathetic light. Quickly springing to mind are the titles *No Survivors*, *Yellow Hair*, *The Brass Command*, *The Squaw Killers*, *Pillars of the Sky*, *From Where the Sun Now Stands*, *The Gates of the Mountains*, and *The Apache Kid*. But Allen also wrote solid fiction about horsemen and their gallant mounts, good men/bad men, men at war, and seeking gold. Ride on.

Chapter Four

Horsemen

Early in his career, before he had well begun to exploit his pro-Indian proclivities, Allen started to demonstrate amazing versatility. His third book was *Wolf-Eye*, the biography of a dog, for children. His fourth book, *Santa Fe Passage*, concerns non-Indian activity along the early Santa Fe Trail. His eighth novel, *The Fourth Horseman*, concerns a would-be horse breeder stumbling into an all-white Arizona feud. Next, in *The Raiders*, Allen turned to the legend of Jesse James. His tenth book, *The Tall Men* (1954), starts his saga of Ben Allison.

So we can see that during his first half-decade of productivity Allen wrote not only about Indians in Red Cloud's country and elsewhere but also about animals, commerce in the Southwest, bad men, and cowboys. This fecundity, more than hinted at early, continued in succeeding decades, as the novelist concerned himself with more horses and with other animals as well, more gunmen, and then war, gold seekers, contemporary outlaws and even future-epoch renegades, as well as still more Indians.

Heroes and Horses

Four of Allen's novels fall into an uneasy group through being concerned with commercial wagoning, would-be horse breeding, gallant horseback riding, and horse-herd driving.

Santa Fe Passage (1952). This novel has been one of Allen's most popular works, although it is not especially challenging to the critic. In it Allen moves back to May 1839 and gives us his first mountain man in Kirby Randolph. (A year later mountain man Joshua Kelso would appear in *Yellow Hair*, already discussed.) Like Kelso, Kirby also moves, in his case south of his northwestern ranges to St. Louis with a load of furs. In *Santa Fe Passage* Allen uses the stock character of the hero's sidekick for his first time. The man is Sam Beekman, whose memories go back to Manuel Lisa and August

44

Pierre Chouteau, and who is now old at fifty. In addition we have a stock character Allen has shown us before—another half-breed, this one in the lovely form of Aurelie St. Clair (French-Apache), whose teeth are so snow white (like Star's in *No Survivors*) and whose smile so resembles heat lightning that Kirby ought to define her as quickly as we do: she is a human embodiment of his adored West.

Dramatic tension must be provided during the time Kirby bosses a wagon train from Westport to Santa Fe. So his prejudice causes him to delay crossing the color line to amour longer than it should. He also must counter villainies along the trail which are caused by wagon-boss Tuss McLawry and by a human enigma—a New Mexican hidalgo named Don Pedro Armijo, company boss of the caravan, nephew of Governor Armijo of the territory of New Mexico, and associate of Colonel Juan Vicarrez. Young Armijo is fast with his guns and knows right away that he wants foxy Aurelie. Kirby also must contend with a Pawnee-built prairie fire, a buffalo stampede engineered by real-life Kiowa hero Satank, and a rousing Indian abduction sequence. Even nature proves inimical and throws violent rain, murderous "buffler" gnats, and desert thirst at the wagoners.

The first part of the novel is epic in its episodic romance and can be mapped along the historic Santa Fe Trail: Westport, Council Grove, Diamond Spring, the Little Arkansas, the Lower Cimarron, and at last Bent's Fort. Here we arrive at Blunt's Fort, however, established by Allen's fictitious firm of Blunt and St. Clair, and paralleling the historical firm of Bent, St. Vrain and Company. During much of the second part of the story Kirby scouts on ahead, falls into the clutches of a Comanche kidnapper named Big Foot, who is aided by one Chavez, and must escape to warn the wagon party, which is already in some measure disloyal to him.

Historical background, though in evidence, is minor in *Santa Fe Passage*. It comes mostly from Josiah Gregg's two-volume classic, *Commerce of the Prairies* (1844).[1] Gregg tells about wagons setting out from Council Grove in May (of 1831, also in April 1839), Governor Armijo and both his nephew Chavez and his associate Colonel Vizcarra, a prairie fire and a Pawnee attack, and Comanche kidnappers. A gory act in *Santa Fe Passage* is Kirby's valiant but fatal amputation of a wagoner's right leg, arrowed and turned gangrenous. In Gregg, the arm-wounded patient survived amputation.[2]

It is easy to see why this novel sold well from the first. Its narrator is ribald and raucous. He portrays a versatile mountain man hero, whose fight against falling in love with a feisty teen-aged half-breed beauty the reader enjoys watching him lose, and whose ability to meet every crisis the reader almost envies. The most memorable feature, however, is not narrator, macho hero, or natural female, but nature itself. Ah, read this:

Late May, warm, the moon fat and just edging up behind the sandhills beyond the crossing. The air tepid and fragrant and just moving enough to bring a prairie man the smells he lived on. Warm sand, new grass, old hay, gray sage, fresh water, damp loam, naked rocks, willow pungence, woodsmoke and simple ozone. Just pure, unadulterated prairie air. Air that got down in a man and tasted so mouth-watering good he would swear he had eaten his belly full of it, instead of just breathing it into his lungs.[3]

Surely here the goal of the trail is the trail.

The Fourth Horseman (1954).   *The Fourth Horseman*, another early novel, illustrates Allen's basic method applied virtually to perfection. The historical event providing the background and foreground of this dark, brooding book is the Graham-Tewksbury feud in Arizona in the 1880s.

As seasoned history buffs will recall, this feud pitted John Tewksbury and his three half-breed sons, Edwin, John, Jr., and James, against Thomas Graham and his brother John. Both clans rustled from their Pleasant Valley neighbors, but the Grahams then kept the ill-gotten herd and thus gained solitary financial eminence. Seeking to get even, the Tewksburys brought thousands of sheep into the cattlemen's valley, with the financial assistance of the Daggs brothers of Flagstaff. The consequent slaughter of innumerable woollies soon escalated into murder. The Grahams seemed unstoppable, especially when backed, as they soon were, by the guns of Mark Blevans's five sons, Mark, Charlie, John, Sam, and Hampton. Old Mark's disappearance prompted one son, Hampton, to gather some friendly Hash Knife gang members and call on Jim Tewksbury, perhaps with innocent intentions. Ambivalent but deadly gunfire erupted and soon the valley became soaked in blood. Uninvolved young William Graham, recently down from Iowa, was shot by Jim Houck, a pro-Tewksbury deputy sheriff from Apache County. Tom Graham, the murdered lad's irate brother, collected all available gunmen and raided the Tewksbury homestead, killed several men, and would not even allow the pinned-down survivors to drive a pack of ravenous hogs from the corpses.

Next, Apache County sheriff Commodore Perry Owens got into the act against the Blevans brothers, whereupon Yavapai County sheriff William Mulvenson (or Mulvenon) decided to stop the feud by arresting rival ringleaders. Some members of the Graham-Blevans faction tried to resist—and died trying. The Tewksbury boys sensibly agreed to be jailed. Temporary peace then followed but was shattered by the ambush of a pro-Graham man, a trial of some Tewksbury boys, though without verdict—because of a shortage of witnesses—senseless lynchings, and midnight disappearances.[4]

And how did Allen convert this material into yet another action novel? He did three significant things. First, he introduced a fictional character named Frank Rachel, based slightly on real-life *pistolero* James F. "Fighting Jim" Roberts (A to G, 4/6/82). Frank is a gunfighter, ever reluctant now and trying to remain retired, who rides into Peaceful Basin in 1882 seeking only quiet work and lasting friendship. His long-range ambition is to raise horses, with the help of his magnificent stud Red Boy. Second, Allen as usual chose to support the less popular side of the feud: *The Fourth Horseman* is pro-Tewksbury. Naturally Frank Rachel, though hoping to remain neutral, is drawn to the Tewksbury family and soon opposes the Grahams and the Blevanses. And third, for dramatic tightness Allen stops his narrative short (in September 1887) and thus does not fictionalize Tom Graham's murder (in August 1892) by Ed Tewksbury, who was tried but acquitted (in February 1895).

Allen changes most key names, but only slightly. Note John, Ed, John, Jr., and Jim Fewkes; Tom and Judd Graden; the Skaggs brothers; Mark Bivins; and Perry Odens and Bill Mulvehey. More than twenty other names can be linked to real-life originals. The novelist ingeniously arranges for Frank Rachel to enter the valley: he tells original-settler James F. "Old Jim" Stanton (really Jim Stinson, victim of the Graham-Tewksbury rustlers) that the old man's wild young nephew is dead. It seems that Frank innocently came upon the lad wounded by a posse, which shot at Frank, who shot back—so effectively that he had to ride for his life to this safely isolated basin near Holbrook, in Arizona Territory. Old Stanton takes note of the horseman's stud Red Boy, whereupon Frank reveals that he was still earlier railroaded to jail by a man who stole this very horse; but Frank escaped, killed the thief and will now watch the recovered stud jealously. Allen provides the Fewkes brothers with a sister named Libby, aged seventeen, violently sexy, tragically unstable. Frank curiously associates his feeling toward sensual women with the forsworn thrill of gunplay. So he resists Libby all he can; but soon he falls, only to become a loner when the girl, now the object of his honest devotion, runs off with a fictional relative of the "Gradens" named Garth Graden. Frank trails them for an inartistically long time (early 1884 to late 1885), gives up, then learns that Libby has been abandoned by Garth and is working as a prostitute, though sick, in Tombstone's notorious Bird Cage, brings her home (December 1886), and cares for her tenderly until she dies (August 1887).

Ever-increasing friendship with the remaining Fewkses makes Frank sympathetic to their sheep venture, even as hatred of Garth makes him forget his neutrality and declare war on all Gradens. Allen is now not only amanuensis as history follows its bloody path but also novelist as he stages the showdown between Frank and Garth. The climax is neatly unforeshadowed and involves Red Boy, the stud, whom Allen endows with a personality all his own. Red Boy must be nominated as the closest thing to a hero in the entire novel.

Allen complicates his narrating of *The Fourth Horseman* by suggesting that it is based on previously unrevealed memoirs and letters from Jim Stanton's niece, who before her death sent the novelist her papers. Allen also provides a map of Arizona Territory which combines real geography and fictional details.[5]

The Blue Mustang (1956). In this action novel the young narrator, Walker "Button" Starbuck, has to ride 175 miles from Dallas to Mason City, Texas, from May 4 to May 6, 1876, with $25,000 in gold (heavy then), to purchase a contracted-for herd of cattle. If he does not arrive in time, he will lose his father's ranch. To make it he must not simply accomplish a long ride but also avoid an assortment of obstacles both human and natural in his path. One reviewer objected to "the considerable dose of nick of timing which gets our young hero out of one impossible corner after another."[6] Perhaps, but most readers are doubtless caught up in the rapid pace of the entire rat-a-tat tale.

Button is only seventeen years old, has two older, tougher brothers, and learns after chapter 2 that his widower father has been cruelly murdered, so that a cattle sale hurtful to the known but shadowy villain will not be consummated. The villain's gunslingers kill Doak, one of Button's brothers, in chapter 8 (at North Fork) and the second, Brack, in chapter 16 (at Lampasas)—with mathematical precision in the thirty-two-chapter novel.

Most of the second half of the novel describes Button's getting the gold from a Dallas bank, buying a tough little blue Mexican mustang, and galloping to success. But the second half also features a confusion of episodes: Button too luckily outwits members of the villain's gang, holes up in a *jacal* to make comically reluctant love with a gorgeous Hispanic-Apache teen-ager, and watches a surrogate father serve a warrant with deadly courage.

Like *Santa Fe Passage, The Gates of the Mountains,* and a few other novels by Allen, *The Blue Mustang* is a journey story—this one of mini-epic proportions. But more significant than plot elements are three aspects of characterization: Button's Huck Finn-like verve. his accepting Brack's deathbed apology and praise, and especially the stamina of Galivanito (Little Hawk), the blue mustang. Telling his own story, Button often sounds like Mark Twain's orphan: "I didn't dast open my mouth for the first few steps back up the street toward the stage depot. But about halfway there, the lonesomes got the best of me and I tried him [a deputy sheriff] out a little."[7] Then "I told him a straight whopper about how Dad had thought we would maybe run into trouble. . . . I kept getting in deeper and deeper, the whole thing tasting fishier by the mouthful—even to me" (100, 101). And "I told her I was a poor orphan Mexican-American boy from Goliad, going west to look for work . . . on one of the big gringo ranches" (118). A frontier doctor has to tell the lad that Brack is dying. Allen explains that "being simply western man enough not to try making a patchwork of empty words" (87), the sawbones blurts out, " 'Don't be afraid, boy . . . *He isn't* " (88). The intense farewell follows. Allen opens his page-long description of Galivanito thus: "He was the sorriest-looking horse ever foaled north of Ciudad Juarez. But he was pure Spanish and of the breed the *mesteñeros* swore would die before they tired. Everything about him was right to my eye" (115)—including his thirteen-hand height, less than seven-hundred-pound weight, straight head, wide eyes, short ears, barrel belly, thick fore- and hind-quarter bones, ewe neck, ribbiness and scars, knocked hip on one side and stiff hock opposite, but mostly his *grullo* color of slatey blue, with dorsal stripe and barred legs and especially "the rare crossline over the shoulders to make the *cruz* of the

Christ-marked Mexican burros—a marking that in the Spanish mind stamped him as 'un caballo de caballos—a horse among horses' " (115). Galivanito is the hero in title and in reality.

The donnée for The Blue Mustang was an event in the career of a cowman named W. B. Slaughter, who in 1873 when he was twenty-three years old rode a wiry Spanish roan through rough territory hiding even rougher men. He covered 130 indirect miles to Mason, carrying 104 pounds of gold pieces worth $25,000, to pay cash and thus consummate a profitable deal on a herd of steers previously contracted for.[8] It is fascinating to compare Slaughter's undramatic, bare-bones story with Allen's dramatic heightening of it. In each account we have advisory banker, disguise by sorry-looking clothes, purchase of ugly-looking Spanish pony, gunmen checking stagecoach, and alibi. Note that Allen works Slaughter's rehearsed story—"If I met any stranger I was to pass as a green youth from Gonzales looking for a job with a trail herd"[9]—into his young hero's Huck-like lie about being a Goliad lad seeking ranch work.

The Bear Paw Horses (1973).   This late novel is one of Allen's most curious and complex works. Further, like Chiricahua, it provides a fine introduction to his varied production. It is a kind of Allen anthology, since it partly repeats earlier material. For example, he again describes the death of Crazy Horse, which he presented in both No Survivors and Custer's Last Stand. The book also repeats many details of the surrender of Chief Joseph, already given in From Where the Sun Now Stands. And the plot of The Bear Paw Horses displays the careful tangle of action for which Chiricahua and Tayopa! (to be considered later) are notable.

An almost unbelievable cast of named characters is offered in The Bear Paw Horses. More than thirty hostile Indians either appear or are reported to be busy not far away. In addition eight named Indians scout for the army, while about fifteen named army officers and men figure in the action, as well as a full half-dozen white civilians.

But the real heroes and heroines are four-footed. They include the magnificent titular herd of 250 surrendered Oglala Sioux horses. It seems that an eighty-year-old Sioux medicine priest named Kangisiha (Crowfoot), his seventeen-year-old granddaughter H'Tayetu (Twilight), who is Crazy Horse's sister-in-law, and a ten-year-old Oglala orphan boy named Tuweni Oyuspi (Nobody Catches Him, i.e., no one can trip him up mentally) adopt Crazy Horse's plan to recapture this herd from a white horse thief named Con Jenkins and drive it from his holding area, near Fort Robinson in western Nebraska, northwest through Wyoming to far Montana. The hope is to deliver the herd to Chief Joseph so that he need not surrender to One Hand Howard. There are other four-footed characters. Old Crowfoot's mule Red Weasel is faithful and enduring. Specklebird is the Indian trio's bellwether she-horse. Lucifer is a big bay owned by V. T. McGillycuddy, the real-life sympathetic white physician at Spotted Tail's agency east of the fort, and "loaned" by the good doctor to Tuweni Oyuspi for the drive. A murdered army deserter's empty-saddled horse enables Crazy Charley Beckwourth, old scout Jim Beckwourth's once-tortured and now demented son, to escape and join the Bear Paw herd. Even Joseph's "premier [Appaloosa] mounts . . . Ebenezer, his war horse, and Ebenezer's half-brother Joshua, the Sunday or show-off horse of the Nez Perce chief,"[10] are vital to the action. The leader loans them to a keen-eyed young scout (really Heyets, narrator of *From Where the Sun Now Stands*) and a fast-riding, tall Indian girl, to spy on Bear Coat Miles's troop movements. Yes, the heroes of *The Bear Paw Horses* are non-human. And the finest effect in the entire book comes when those gallant Indian ponies, racing along parallel to the Bozeman Trail and then narrowing toward it, cross into Montana and smell freedom on the wind.

Allen manages scene shifts and plot weavings with great skill here. Crazy Horse (until he dies), Crowfoot, and Twilight appear in twenty-five chapters. Tuweni figures in fifteen, at first away from Crowfoot and Twilight, then with them, and often alone again later, or captured by the enemy. Con Jenkins the white rustler is in thirteen chapters, at first with his renegade crew but later with Crowfoot and Twilight, whom he joins and one of whom he ultimately loves.[11] Chief Joseph appears in seven chapters, only one of them with Crowfoot, Twilight, Con, and Tuweni. Crazy Charley weaves in and out of sixteen chapters, first with Con, then alone, later actively, still later passively. Maggart, nicknamed Maggot, the crooked deserter, disgraces four chapters. Army chief of scouts Captain Terrance Smith South, or at least his scouts, figure in only five chapters but with plot-wrenching violence.[12]

All of this is to suggest that in *The Bear Paw Horses* Allen reveals masterful handling of some seven separate and intertwining plot strands. He provides a better metaphor: "*Iktomi*, the Sioux call them. They are the tiny spidermen who . . . weave the web of sorrows that entraps the lives of men, tumbling all toward the center of the web with an ever-increasing speed. This web was closing now upon the scattered ones whose lives were caught within the war-chief's [Crazy Horse's] dream of freedom" (142); and later "[t]he spidermen now spun the last of the web that was to be the story of the Bear Paw horses. Only they, the *iktomi* of Sioux folklore, knew the ending. Their tiny hands flew faster, faster, for what they saw was darkness coming down. And the horses of the warchief's dream were still not met with the Slit Nose [Nez Percé] brother [Joseph]" (194).[13]

The "scattered ones," including the remnant of the exhausted pony herd, all tumble together in the fatal Bear Paw Mountains of what is now north-central Montana on the night of October 5, 1877. The Oglala trio, abetted by Con, might have failed by the mean judgments of white-man history, but they succeeded by Indian standards of the spirit. Sioux tradition insists that the epic gallop was not in vain, because, in the dead of that ghastly October night, untamable Yellow Wolf and aged Chief White Bird broke Joseph's selfless surrender pledge and, mounting their followers on the 113 surviving Oglala horses, escaped with seventy-eight Nez Percé men, women, and children to Canada, safe at last and still free people.

Perhaps too much happens in this busy novel, as Allen mixes white history, Indian tradition, and melodramatic fiction. The plot might well have started after Crazy Horse's death; perhaps fewer obstacles might have blocked the horse-herd path, for aesthetic crispness. Plans fail. Deaths occur. Much heroism goes for naught. But that gallant herd smelled freedom for one grand moment.

Saga of the Tall Man

In 1954 Allen published *The Tall Men*, the first volume of what became a five-volume saga mostly starring Ben Allison (already discussed in connection with *Apache Ransom*). The later titles are *The Big Pasture, Return of the Tall Man, Outcasts of Canyon Creek*, and *Apache Ransom*. To complicate matters, *Outcasts of Canyon Creek* is partly a continuation of an earlier vigilante novel, entitled *Reckoning at Yankee Flat* (to be considered later), while *Black Apache* (also to be treated later), mostly a story about a fabulous lost gold mine, includes several characters from *Apache Ransom* and also even introduces Ben's lost sister Stella Allison.

It was undoubtedly the phenomenal sales success of *The Tall Men*, together with its sale to Hollywood for film adaptation in 1955, that prompted Allen to write its sequel quickly; the open-ended conclusion of *The Tall Men*, however, had already left the novelist with the option of a second volume. Perhaps he saw at once the durability of his hero Ben, who is surely still alive and well "out there."

The Tall Men (1954).   *The Tall Men* is mostly fiction, but it has a central character based on a real-life figure. Allen's Nathan Stark, who wants to make a quick million dollars selling Texas cattle in Montana, owes a great deal to history's once-famous Nelson Story, who like Stark defied foul weather, hostile Indians, and overly protective soldiers from Fort Phil Kearny to get his first herd up to Bozeman City, Montana, in December 1866, and thus make a financial killing.[14]

The Tall Men starts in Virginia City, Montana, in February 1866, as Stark is being robbed of $40,000, which he wants to spend in Texas on cheap livestock. The would-be robbers are a pair of brothers named Ben and Clint Allison. They are tall Texans, one-quarter Kwahadi Indian, tough, with cold eyes, fast of movement. They are also down-and-out Confederate army veterans. Stark persuades them to return his money and throw in with him on his venture. On their way to Texas they encounter some starving immigrants and save the prettiest of them—lovely young Texan Nella Torneau—from a Sioux attack led by one Tashunka Witko, whose name is tardily translated, six chapters later, for maximum emphasis. He is Crazy Horse! With Nella in tow, Stark and his party get to Fort Worth, pick up three thousand head of cattle and a motley crew (partly out of a Hollywood casting office, I'd say), and head 'em north at the precise halfway point of the novel.

The second half is an epic of timed-release challenges somewhat like those of *Santa Fe Passage.* Here our tall men face dreary rain, Jayhawkers demanding toll money, Indian attacks, and Colonel Carrington's order not to proceed north of Fort Reno. But the cowpokes push on anyway, to victory and financial reward for Stark, albeit at a fearful cost in human life when their passage is contested by Indians on November 23, 1866, where the Bozeman crosses the Yellowstone.

Dramatic tension is intensified by three means. First, Nella sleeps with Ben to pay him for saving her life—"'A woman like me's got only one way to pay a man she's beholden to,'"[15] she says unnecessarily, because Ben is smitten for good. She later imagines a more secure future with Stark but finally opts for Ben again. Second, Clint

Allison recognizes Stark's shady selfishness whereas his brother Ben is more trusting. For a wary, Indian-like cowboy, hero Ben is curiously naïve at times. Further, Clint from the beginning seems branded by fate for death. And third, Stark is oddly schizoid, being strong but aloof, demanding but unsure, generous but mean.

The tragic tone in *The Tall Men* is mitigated by occasional raucous ribaldry. The most uproarious example comes when Clint, ordered by Ben to listen up, says, " 'Ears widespread as handles on a slop-jar. . . . Pick me up and pee me full' " (91; see also 137). Much of the humor is reminiscent of parts of *Red Blizzard*, whose hero Pawnee Perez, in fact, puts in a brief appearance here. Clayton, known as Cetan Mani, is also mentioned and his activities are discussed.

In a charming epilogue Allen distances his narration into misty legend when he reports that famed Cheyenne chief Two Moons, while reminiscing at the Lame Deer, Montana, agency in 1915, remembered one of tall Stark's gallant crew as the tallest of them all. He was Ben. Beginning with a prefatory report of Stark's "princely wealth" (no p.), the novel rightly focuses on quietly heroic Ben Allison at fade-out time.

The Big Pasture (1955). *The Big Pasture* is a disappointing sequel to *The Tall Men*. It begins well enough. The time is mid-December 1866, the place Virginia City; and cattleman Nathan Stark—now called Nathan Mason Stark—is paying his crew, which includes tall Ben, who has won Nella, now pregnant by him, and who starts with her for home in Texas with two cowpoke friends. They are Chickasaw Billings and Waco Fentriss, both of whom could have been played by Gabby Hayes. Twin disasters strike: Ben is lost in a landslide, and Stark's breeding herd is lost in a blizzard. Nella, who is ignorant of his financial ruin, returns resignedly to Stark, who is ignorant of her pregnancy. For selfish and vengeful purposes, each agrees to marry the other; but then each learns the truth about the other. The only immediate good result is that the Texas crew, including some cronies of Chickasaw and Waco, agree to remain with Stark for the sake of Mrs. Stark's baby by "dead" Ben.

The rest of *The Big Pasture* is improbable if exciting. The cowboys save most of the snowbound herd and drive it into a secret valley—in the breathtaking Upper Gallatin—where they hole up until June 1867, fight off a band of murderous but stupid Crows, and win out by standing them off until troopers from Fort Ellis charge to a Hollywood rescue.

Highlights include General Grant, an old herd bull with a heifer harem; a pathetic Indian woman whose story, which she tells to Nella, parallels the white girl's history and thus offers her a timely moral lesson (accept love now); mention of our old friend Cetan Mani from *No Survivors*, during an Indian visitor's gossip around a campfire; and—above all—Esau Lazarus (introduced in *The Tall Men*), a wise old Jewish business friend[16] who admonishes Stark early in the novel with such vigor that he can compliment the changed man at the end. But *The Big Pasture* shows signs of haste.

Return of the Tall Man (1961). This novel is better than *The Big Pasture*; in fact, it is one of Allen's most remarkable efforts. The tall man who returns is Ben. The landslide did not kill him after all. But it did give him amnesia, a misfortune which costs him Nella and their son.

The plot is as episodic as Henry Fielding's *Tom Jones* and falls into thirds, as do Tom's picaresqueries. Further, the movement is like that of a typical modern detective novel, each episode giving clues leading to the next action. Ben is pulled from the landslide by an old prospector named Chilkoot Johnston on December 10, 1866. Chilkoot nurses him to some degree of health at his shack on Nameless Creek. But Ben has amnesia and $10,000 in a money belt—his payoff from *The Tall Men*. Chilkoot first tells him that Ben will be accused by the vigilantes of the recent murder of a man for *his* $10,000 and second gives him an old map and persuades him to go find his daughter Amy Johnston, abducted by Utah Paiutes back in '43.

The odyssey begins. Ben seeks not only Amy but his own past. One way to describe his slapdash acts is to say that in chapter after chapter he meets a stranger, who may or may not prove helpful, but whose contribution is to impel him onward. Chapter 3—old Paiutes give Ben leads to Amy's Shoshone abductor. Chapter 4—Milk River half-breed joins Ben, aids him. Chapter 6—Christian agency Nez Percé joins both, aids them, says he long has loved Amy. Chapter 10—Crazy Horse and Cetan Mani reveal Amy traded to Satank, then give boy guide to Ben's party south to Kiowas Satank, Satanta, Big Tree. Chapter 12—guide betrays them to Kiowas. Chapter 13—Canadian scout for army saves Ben and friends, says Amy sold to Comancheros. Chapter 16—Ben's party find Comancheros, see Amy. Chapter 18—Amy sold to Broken Hand, friend of Mimbreños Apache Mangas Coloradas the younger; Ben and party tortured in camp of Quanah Parker, who returns, sees Ben's Kwahadi Comanche water-horse tattoo, spares all. Chapter 21—Quanah Parker provides scout to lead Ben's party into Apacheria. Chapter 23—Ben's party captured by Broken Hand. Chapter 24—Ben's party see Amy again. Chapters 26 and 27—Ben and party escape with Amy. Chapter 31—Ben's party kill many Apache would-be ambushers. Chapter 33—Ben, Amy, and friends return to Montana, sort out lives; Ben falls, cracks head, regains memory in Stark's presence, learns Nella died in childbirth; Amy honors father, marries Ben's Nez Percé Christian friend, adopts Ben's son.

Reduced to plot summary, *Return of the Tall Men* sounds a bit grotesque. But on first reading it has force and sweep, and robust humor. On second reading its clever construction becomes more apparent. The book falls into almost equal thirds (chapters 1-10, 11-20, 21-31) and a coda. In chapter 10 Ben meets Crazy Horse and Cetan Mani, who send him on. In chapter 20 Ben is saved by Quanah Parker, who sends him on. In chapter 31 Ben and his fellow survivors so act as to assure victory. Ben experiences glimmerings from his past—familiarity with guns, knowledge of Spanish, details of former work, awareness of Indian ways—which light his darkened memory and help pace the narrative. It is exciting the way Allen causes real-life characters to pop into the action: Crazy Horse, Washakie, Satank and his friends, Quanah Parker, and Mangas Coloradas the younger. Even Allen's creation, durable Cetan Mani, has a cameo reappearance. Allen twice uses the reverse of foreshadowing: at the end of chapter 10 he tells us flatly that Ben never again "saw or heard of the tall, gray-eyed Oglala [Cetan Mani],"[17] and at the end of chapter 20 he reports that Ben "never saw Quanah Parker again" (126). Once the gunsmoke clears at the end of chapter 31, a friend says, " 'Brother Ben, . . . [l]et's go' " (187), and the rest is peacefully sentimental.

A curious feature of *Return of the Tall Man* is the combination of references in it to a number of other Allen books: at least ten of them could be shown to intersect with this one. What is more, at the very end Ben is defined—"the Tall Man who returned from death to ride out his life in the service of his brothers . . . who had not his strength to serve themselves" (200)—so as to point toward his next mission, which is to help a victim of vigilante injustice.

Outcasts of Canyon Creek (1972).   This novel, one of Allen's weakest, is the least satisfactory of the five Tall Man volumes. It is a mishmash of melodramatics and improbabilities. It delineates the antics of Ben Allison, who while in danger of being lynched in 1868 by corrupt vigilantes out of Virginia City and Canyon Creek, Montana, for a robbery and murder he did not commit, avoids the temptation to sneak off to Texas and home but instead rescues a mistrustful teen-aged mulatto lad wrongly accused of axing a white girl to death. In mid-flight the two escapees decide to return, after all, to Virginia City and clear their names. In the process they kill a few men in self-defense, join a proscribed prostitute friend of the dead girl, unmask a demented gold miner long disguised as the region's crippled hunchback, and even discover not only that the axe murderer is the vigilante chief himself but also that he is the long-lost daddy of the mulatto—who when he completes his perilous "search for the father" wishes that he had not.

Outcasts of Canyon Creek is also disfigured as to structural shape. The first part has a measured gait, occurs in one locale, and has painstakingly reported action of an almost believable sort: escape, parley, hide, fight, deceive, succeed. But the second half features dime-novel events composed in a different key altogether: the pageant-like exodus from town of the over-the-hill prostitute, three brutal murders in back-to-back chapters, a crawl through a bat- and rat-infested mine tunnel, a slide down a mill chute, pusillanimities of timorous townspeople, and even Ben's firing a dummy of himself at the armed villain by aspen-tree catapult. At the end we learn what happens to the villain, the hero, and his friends only by offstage and epilogical reporting.

The best part of the novel is the terminal hint that obscure Ben Allison, home at last in his beloved hot Texas, may already have accepted the governor's commission to descend into the Apaches' Sierra Madre fortress and arrange for the release of the governor's kidnapped son. But, as Allen says, *"hay historia otra del todo."*[18] Yes, indeed—another story. And its name is *Apache Ransom*, considered in chapter 3.

It should be mentioned that *Outcasts of Canyon Creek* has links to Montana history, although Allen's interest in vigilantism is displayed more thoroughly in his earlier and better *Reckoning at Yankee Flat*. A vigilante named John X. Beidler in that book becomes F. X. Reedler in *Outcasts of Canyon Creek*; both are based on real-life Montana vigilante John Xavier Beidler.[19] The irrepressible Allen bases another name in *Outcasts of Canyon Creek* on a historical figure. The name of old Judge Larned Handleman of Bozeman, Montana, in Allen's fiction must owe something to that of the later, more Eastern Learned Hand.

Allen's eight novels about horses and their tall riders reveal his love of horses, ponies, and even mules. In addition, the novelist dramatizes the values of courage, tenacity, and laconism. For the critical reader, what is proved here again is the difficulty of dividing Allen's novels into classes with any hope of being tidy. Time after time a given story intersects both with another story and also with a piece of history overlapping another piece of history occasioning yet another story.

Chapter Five

Good Men / Bad Men

As important in Allen's production as his novels about clashes between Indians and the army, and those about horsemen and their noble mounts, are his several books about legendary good men branded as evil and bad men labeled good. Crotchety Allen's formula is almost predictable. Jesse James and the Younger brothers have been equated with Robin Hood and his merry men? Kill the legend. Wyatt Earp has been downgraded as a thug? Romanticize him. Butch Cassidy, Ned Huddleston (alias Isom Dart), and Tom Horn were common gunmen? Depict them as funny, stoical, amorous; treat them sympathetically. Henry Plummer was a cold-blooded, hypocritical killer? Yes, but at least endow him with a satanic glitter. Vigilantism was finally wrong? Oh, was it? Texas cattle rustlers deserved to be strung up without exception? Wait; examine the childhood and formative years of a typical one.

Heroes?

The Raiders (1954).   Rightly pleased with *The Fourth Horseman*, his first novel to feature all-white violence, Allen next turned to an even more violent all-white story—the legend of Jesse James. *The Fourth Horseman* was published in May 1954. In September of the same year appeared *Death of a Legend*, the true account of the James and Younger brothers. A couple of years later it was innocuously retitled *The Raiders*.

Instead of investing history with fictive trappings, as he had done with the Graham-Tewksbury feud for *The Fourth Horseman*, Allen in *The Raiders* reduced legend to matter-of-fact reportorial literature. To be sure, he opens the story of cold-hearted Jesse with a largely imaginative episode in his childhood. Jesse callously kills an old bluetick hound while he, his older brother Frank James, and their crony young Cole Younger are recapturing a freed slave in Centerville, Missouri, on May 27, 1856. We dislike Jesse from that moment

59

on.[1] Naturally, Allen also invents a great deal of dialogue, much of it designed to set Jesse's inhumanity against Cole Younger, who comes off as huge and brave, loyal and stoical by comparison.

After the 1856 incident Allen carries us forward to 1863 with a debunking account of Jesse James's Civil War guerrilla activities under William F. "Bloody Bill" Anderson. The compelling follow-up, though fascinating, lacks the thrill of Allen's more imaginative historomantic renditions. *The Raiders* scrupulously details its nefarious central character's career as it expanded from Clay County, Missouri, to Centralia, Liberty, and Gallatin, and then up and down to Iowa, Texas, Alabama, Kansas City, and fatal Northfield, Minnesota, where on September 7, 1876, the gang tried to rob the First National Bank but was shot to ribbons by an enraged citizenry. The event cost the treacherous James brothers the further services of Cole, Jim, and Bob Younger, whose later careers Allen does not touch on. After a period of pseudonymous quiet in Nashville, Tennessee, Jesse and a new gang returned to Missouri train robbing. Their bloody conduct prompted the offering of rewards which Bob Ford could not resist.

Allen faithfully includes anti-establishment commentary and depicts the Pinkerton bloodhounds as sufficiently slavering, but his avowed purpose is to revise "the persistently misrepresented life of a cold-blooded killer."[2] Jesse James is almost tediously depicted as watery of eye, savage of temper, fast as a snake, and with uncanny powers of leadership. His marriage to his cousin Zerelda Mimms is unlovely in the extreme, apart from her skewed loyalty. Allen as narrator, with objectivity but also irony, varies the movement of time, often giving us dates directly, sometimes hinting at others, presenting some events straight, but many others retrospectively.

The book is in three parts, called "Daybreak," "High Noon," and "Nightfall." These parts contain, respectively, four, five, and three chapters. Each chapter has a place name for its title, as though, now that Jesse James is blessedly extinct and the true story of his crimes can be told, only the land he stained need be particularized. Among the best chapters are chapter 7, "Adair," about the first professional train robbery in the world, at Adair, Iowa, on July 21, 1873; and chapter 10, "Northfield."[3] Notable as technical accomplishments are Allen's suggestion that Jesse's story is a kind of cosmic drama and the novelist's cluster of little images to the effect that fate is a female bookkeeper who was relieved when she could close the bloody Missouri gunman's ledger.[4]

Who Rides with Wyatt (1955).   Inevitably, Allen had to write about Wyatt Earp sooner or later. But unlike his chronicle of Jesse James, *Who Rides with Wyatt* is structurally complex and more than half fictional. Allen begins with an immediate challenge to the reader by setting his story in a triple-narrative frame. He ends by teasing the reader with a curious puzzle. In between, he offers a sequence of nicely timed narrative climaxes.

First we are told that a Tombstone desperado told his life's story, which included a connection with Wyatt Earp during the lawman's Arizona days, to a friend who survived to become a Prescott old-timer who told Allen, in 1933, everything which the novelist now proceeds to disclose.

The narrative proper begins in 1880 when Wyatt saves Johnny Ringo from death in a Texas gunfight. The narrative ends with what passes for evil Ringo's corpse found outside Tombstone beside tracks of Wyatt's horse. This clearly implicates the departed hero. Did Wyatt do away with Ringo? Did the ne'er-do-well perhaps kill himself? Was the fellow who became the talkative Prescott old-timer the killer? According to a permissible reading of the finale, Ringo might have shot a decoy and escaped. Or perhaps Wyatt did so, to aid Ringo.[5]

Now, between introduction and ending, *Who Rides with Wyatt* has three distinct climactic sequences. First, there are two central female characters, prim Evelyn "Evvie" Cushman, who runs a proper rooming house, and Lilith "Tombstone Lilly" Beloit, a Bird Cage entertainer. Wyatt cannot decide whether he should love Miss Evvie decorously or quick-like bed down with Lilly lustfully, which latter he does both before and after a comically frustrated proposal of marriage to Evvie. The ironic climax of his carnal relationship with Lilly is their weary, mutual recognition that he will forever carry a pure torch for the prelapsarian Eve of the tale.[6] A second, more gruesome climax is occasioned by the famous shootout at the O.K. Corral, on October 26, 1881, which Allen stages gloriously and all to the credit of Wyatt Earp, his brothers Virgil and Morgan, and their friend John Henry "Doc" Holliday. But then beyond this action, which might have ended the novel, comes its third climax, implacable, lion-like Wyatt's revenge on the Curly Bill Brocius gang, which crippled Virgil and murdered Morgan.

Western buffs will never decide whether Wyatt Earp was a hero or a villain. But Allen, who bridles at the debunking of authentic Western idols, admires Wyatt and says so in no uncertain terms, recently writing thus: "If Frank Waters [anti-Earp author of *The Earp Brothers of Tombstone* (1960)] is anti-Earp, that's all right with me. Crook, liar, thief, poseur, fake, call Old Wyatt anything you like, but don't name him coward or unversed in warfare by the gun. We have too many hero-breakers today. I will continue to defend the myth. Were I to write *Who Rides with Wyatt* today, I would not switch allegiances. Every man was a son of a bitch to someone. Wyatt still stands higher above his bunions than any of his penny-ante detractors. It's all a lot of swine-dip. Long live the legend."[7]

So Allen happily portrays his tall, fair-haired, pale-eyed, mustachio-tugging, lion-voiced Wyatt with respect and verve.[8] And he includes almost as many real-life subordinate actors as people *The Fourth Horseman*, more of them here, however, with their real names intact. We have, for example, J. P. Clum, Johnny Behan, and Ike, Phil, and Billy Clanton, among others already mentioned. In addition, some names are easily recognizable even when altered slightly. For a few examples, history's Fred White becomes Allen's Ferd Wagner, Tom McLaury becomes Tom McLowry, Bob Hatch's saloon becomes Campbell and Hatch's Pool Hall, etc. Thus the novelist finds his stage crowded enough without introducing further complications such as Wyatt's questionable political and commercial activities—all of which might have put feet of clay under a heavy hero of bronze. Three splendid aspects of this fine action novel are Wyatt's heart-warming friendship with a skinny little Mexican kid named Chico Gutierrez, Allen's topographical accuracy, and his clinical description of wounds.

Reckoning at Yankee Flat (1958).   For his next novel about a controversial white gunman, Allen went back more than a decade, north from Arizona to Bannack and Virginia City, Montana, and for inspiration to an early classic of Western biographical history. It is *The Vigilantes of Montana* (1866) by Thomas J. Dimsdale, British-born teacher and newspaper editor who lived in Montana from 1863 until his death of tuberculosis two years later. The leading villain of Dimsdale's history is Henry Plummer—politician, law officer, ladies' man, rapist, multiple murderer, sheriff of Bannack, secret leader of goldfield road agents, and lynch-law victim on January 10, 1864. Plummer is the veritable Satan of *Reckoning at Yankee Flat*, which Allen privately described once as follows: "Best approach yet to Henry Plummer and the Vigilantes of Montana. Practically a screenplay between covers. Great!"[9] Since Allen does not attempt to whitewash a villain or degrade a hero, the novel is virtually unique in his canon.

The narrative is the first-person account of William Cullah "Cul" McCandles and is based, Allen avers, on journalist Cul's handwritten records and notes, "not as yet authenticated."[10] Cul studies Plummer's apprentice-criminal activities in California, graduates to the status of a gun-wise, gold-mining adult himself in the Northwest, and then on his way home to see his widowed mother in Kansas City (he never gets back there) bumps into Plummer again at Fort Benton on the Upper Missouri. Instead of letting himself be killed for his substantial savings, Cul pretends to join Plummer in a criminal foray on Bannack.

Cul is an engaging loser most of the time. Plummer snookers his wildly sexy girlfriend, Electra Bryan, away from him. Cul invests in worthless Montana mines. He goes hunting with the Stuart-Fairweather party but is captured by unfriendly Crows. He learns that wily Plummer has been elected sheriff when he returns to Bannack with his charming Crow mistress, named Lisa after famed Manuel Lisa (mentioned in *Santa Fe Passage*), for whom the girl's grandfather worked long ago. Like other white men in Allen's early fiction, Cul lusts for dark-skinned women but fancies that white ones are safer in the long run. It surprises the reader of unlucky Cul's story to learn that the fellow joins the vigilantes, because doing so could result in the most fatal of his personal losses. But he reports what he knows, becomes a brave follower of mostly real-life vigilante leaders, and—as we know from history—it was Plummer who lost and was destroyed.

Reckoning at Yankee Flat falls into thirds which seem too discrete. The first nine chapters (April 1852 to April 8, 1863) concern Plummer's youth in California and on to the end of his first winter in Bannack; Cul, finding no newspaper work there and losing his money, leaves town to go hunting. The middle nine chapters (to June 25, 1863) ignore Plummer to follow Cul in and out of Indian captivity and also describe the Fairweather gold strike at Alder Gulch, in which Cul undeservedly shares; this section ends with his depositing Lisa for safekeeping with Esau Lazarus (our Jewish friend from *The Tall Men* and *The Big Pasture*). The last nine chapters (to mid-January 1864) counterpoint Plummer's brazen villainy and the vigilantes' determination.

Pretty straight out of "Tom" Dimsdale, who is quoted (as is

Nathaniel Pitt "Nat" Langford's *Vigilante Days and Ways* [1890]),
are D. R. Dillingham's murder, his killers' joke of a trial, the activities of George Ives (a close friend of Cul's) and his associates, and
vigilante action against Plummer and his cohorts Buck Stinson and
Ned Ray, among others. Skillfully intertwined with these dark strands
from history is a lighter skein involving fictitious Cul McCandles.
Allen presumably felt that Plummer by himself could not sustain a
whole novel. But the result is that Plummer disappears from too
much of the narrative, Cul with the Indians seems out of key and not
original enough, and his initial comic tone turns inharmoniously
bitter toward the last. Noteworthy are Allen's inclusion of superlative
details about animals, bad weather, and techniques of trailing and
mining.

In 1972, as noted in the previous chapter, Allen published a
continuation of his *Reckoning at Yankee Flat*. It is *Outcasts of Canyon
Creek*, in which Ben Allison, hero of *The Tall Man* saga, runs afoul
of the Montana vigilantes in 1868, by which time the formerly
admirable vigilantes have become badly led, murderously inclined,
racist, and undeserving of any further reader sympathy.

A Loner

And now for a novel which is unlike any other by Allen. Its hero
is almost as villainous as Jesse James and Henry Plummer but merits
a degree of sympathy from us. And he is as brave and loyal to his
crew as Wyatt Earp and yet may be called depraved. He is totally
fictional Hushton Hatterson "Hush" Feleen[11] of *The Feleen Brand*
(1962). The buried moral of this novel is that a second chance is
useless if you have ruined yourself by spoiling your first chance.
Or perhaps the moral is that a naturalistically determined adverse
fate can really spoil everything for you.

The adventures of Hush the "hero" begin when, as a quiet-spoken
mountain boy, still grieving for his recently dead mother Nancy, he
accompanies his father Jupe from Tennessee to Texas in 1873, only to
see Jupe lynched for rustling a couple of years later. Thereafter,
the young man vows to get revenge by any means. At first the reader
sympathizes with young Hush, who is only eighteen at the time of his
father's death. Hush and his five younger siblings, one a crippled
sister, are adopted by a splendid old Mexican *hombre del monte* who
warns volatile Hush to control his frightful temper—but to no avail.

True, Hush is often an aggrieved party; but he overreacts, whether against a wild steer, Indian horse thieves, or a rich cattleman who rustles Hush's illegally gathered herd. Villains here are villainous, all right, but Allen's anti-hero is likewise. When Hush steals the criminal cattleman's ranch and also his slatternly wife, it is difficult to care about any of these unsavory people. The second half of the novel connects with history through the brief introduction of Charles Goodnight, Tom Horn, Bill Tilghman, Bat Masterson, and Wyatt Earp, and concludes with a picture of Hush both unprincipled and, because he grows demented, also pitiful. The reader of *The Feleen Brand* is whipsawed throughout its precisely equal quarters: Hush is sympathetically depicted in chapters 1-9 (1857 to September 1875), less so in chapters 10-18 (to September 1876), more so in chapters 19-27 (to January 1878), and less so in chapters 28-36 (to October 1880). Hush takes separate lovers in chapters 18, 27, and 33; this helps to unify but also to vibrate the plot.

Near the end Allen assumes a straight face and expresses regret that details are incomplete concerning his hero since Dodge City old-timers can recall only "scattered bits and pieces" of Hush's last visit there before the "folklore trail vanishes altogether."[12] Perhaps, but Hushton Feleen, like Henry Plummer, becomes satanic and hence larger than any human model. What he burns with "the Feleen brand" is mortally stricken.

Three Enigmas

Three fascinating bad men of the Far West were George LeRoy Parker, better known as Butch Cassidy; Ned Huddleston, who inexplicably took the name Isom Dart one day; and enigmatic Tom Horn. All were renegades. Each had his dark side. Through Western mythmaking each is now larger than life.

Alias Butch Cassidy (1967). As in *The Feleen Brand*, great importance is placed on the bad hero's youth in *Alias Butch Cassidy*. Allen carries George LeRoy Parker only to age twenty-one. And once again as in Hush's fable, the mute moral seems to be that when a kid goes wrong he cannot turn the clock back to innocence, any more than F. Scott Fitzgerald's Jay Gatsby could; nor can he ever go home again, any more than Thomas Wolfe's George Webber could.

Alias Butch Cassidy opens with LeRoy, aged sixteen, so bored on his Mormon father Maximilian Parker's Utah ranch in 1882 that he is easily lured into crime by an old cowboy named Mike Cassidy, whose last name the youth later takes. Mike and LeRoy bungle a bank job in nearby Panguitch and are pursued by a suspicious deputy sheriff, whom Mike kills. LeRoy is morally still innocent, but he is now technically a murderer's accomplice—all the more so when he helps Mike, wounded across some ribs, to escape to Robber's Roost. LeRoy too quickly drops Mike to team up with fellow-Mormon Matt Warner, another real-life criminal, only to foil that almost satanic young man's effort to kill a ferryboat operator. Once again, LeRoy then splits off from a dangerous friend.

Allen lets his narrative awkwardly skip ahead four years at this point. We pick up with LeRoy, now calling himself George Cassidy (not "Butch" at all in this novel)[13] and wandering through colorful Telluride, Colorado, where he is spotted by Matt. This nemesis persuades his brother-in-law Tom McCarty, head of the real-life McCarty gang, to force George into another criminal scheme, which he once more foils. Is he still innocent? The novel closes in and out of and beyond Brown's Hole, once a robbers' beautiful hideout—a haven for tough gunmen where Colorado, Utah, and Wyoming meet—which is now Allen's favorite scenic spot on earth (A to G, 7/23/81). Of it the novelist recently wrote: "Brown's Hole was a microcosm of the frontier. A sort of telescoped playing out of the broader drama of the entire west. You can apply what you soak up from [John Rolfe] Burroughs to any part of the west, particularly the northern half of the Great West."[14] At novel's end, late in 1887, Cassidy masterminds another robbery which he again foils when his partners grow too violent to square with his twisted philosophy of conduct.

Such a summary mocks what is a strangely gripping but not a consequential novel. Cassidy is quick-witted, comic and light-hearted most of the time, and enviably forgiving. He keeps his promise, here at least, never to become an owlhoot man, that is, a bloody-handed desperado like Mike. Allen makes Hawthornean comments on the intertwined nature of fate and free will, and also says good things about violence and the temptation of easy money. A novel bent on combining violence frustrated and didacticism skirting the tiresome could have been stodgy. Instead, *Alias Butch Cassidy* is uproariously funny—it is perhaps Allen's most comic novel—though darkened at the last by the young hero's nightmare recollection of that clumsy Panguitch deputy mortally shot by Mike and flopping like a badly butchered animal, before a horrified teenager's very eyes.[15]

One More River to Cross (1967).   Published in the same year as *Alias Butch Cassidy, One More River to Cross* even repeats an admittedly beautiful description of Brown's Hole from the other novel.[16]

One More River to Cross is a mostly veracious reconstruction of the life of Ned Huddleston, alias Isom Dart. At the opening of the novel the Civil War has just broken out and Ned, a twelve-year-old Arkansas slave boy, becomes a forager for his kind Confederate soldier-master. After the war Ned turns into a westering drifter trying poignantly to cross that last river over to true freedom. Astoundingly versatile, he is handyman, wrongly suspected killer, homicidal avenger, outwitter even of Apaches, bold companion of Comancheros and even Comanches, able wild-horse hunter, rustler, cowboy, Brown's Hole habitué, comically ineffective lover, tracker of Indians, dull-witted prisoner of the Shoshones, reformed outlaw, Oklahoma Territory cotton farmer, and blissful but then worried surrogate father of an Indian girl—until 1884.

It is hard to discover any unifying principle behind this picaresque Western. Instead, displaying the Melvillean ragged edge of truth, it twists and sprawls—but excitingly. Physical movement in the action is generally west but not always. Psychological progress is usually toward freedom but with agonizing reverses. Gradually, however, we see that Isom, like Melville's non-whites, consistently avoids initiating evil action himself but only reacts to it when it is caused by others. His kindness to children, to the defenseless, and to animals also becomes predictable. Somewhat unifying too may be Isom's reliance on his juju hunches. Moreover, the reader grows familiar with the buzzard shadow of death that trails Allen's seemingly cursed hero. His final act of forgiveness strikes some as anticlimactic, even smacking of Uncle Tomism on the *llano*. But it is more memorable than any vengeance might be. At the end of *One More River to Cross* Allen's gaunt black Isom Dart—if not history's—is at peace with himself, his memories, the Western land, life in general, and God.

Isom Dart was not the first black character in Allen's fiction. Blacks appeared in three earlier novels—*The Seven Men at Mimbres Springs, San Juan Hill* (to be discussed later), and *The Gates of the Mountains*. And Isom would not be the last. Blacks also figure in the post-1967 *See How They Run* (to be treated subsequently), *Outcasts of Canyon Creek, Summer of the Gun* (also to be considered later), and—as already seen—*Apache Ransom* and *Black Apache*. But with

Robert E. Lee Flicker of the two *Apache* titles just named, and per-
haps York of *The Gates of the Mountains*, Isom Dart is one of
Allen's most significant blacks and is brilliantly characterized in *One
More River to Cross*.[17]

I, Tom Horn (1975).   Allen chose not to continue historo-
manticizing the life of Isom Dart beyond the year 1884, for two
good reasons. First, in real life Isom picked up with cattle-rustler
Matt Rash, who in Allen's novel villainously seduces Isom's adopted
Indian daughter, stabs a friend who alerts Isom, and abandons the
girl on the prairie when she is dying of smallpox. And second, in
real life both Matt and Isom ignored the warning of a cattlemen's
detective calling himself James Hicks to stop their rustling and get
out of Brown's Park (formerly the Hole). Refusing, both were shot
to death—Matt on July 8, 1900; Isom on October 3, 1900. Hicks
was really Tom Horn, suspected of both killings.[18] Allen wished to
make separate heroes out of Isom Dart and Tom Horn, and a villain,
or at least a weakling, out of Matt Rash. So it would not have done
to carry *One More River to Cross* into the year 1900.

I, Tom Horn is Allen's finest novel with a white hero. It is divided
chronologically into three books, each of the last two being relentlessly longer than the one before. Every one of its fifty-five chapters
has a two-word title. The cumulative effect of this technique is very
pleasant.

The first book takes Tom Horn from age fourteen, in Missouri, in
1874, southwest through Kansas City and Newton, Kansas, to Santa
Fe and Prescott, in 1876. The second book is devoted to Horn's
decade among the Apaches on the San Carlos reservation and south
into Old Mexico's Chihuahua and Sonora, partly on the trail of
elusive Geronimo. Most of the time during Book Two, Horn is an
aide to famed army scout Al Sieber, whom we met briefly in *The
Apache Kid*. Most of the action here may be dated 1876-86, but the
narrative is carried into the year 1890. The third book moves north
to Colorado and then fatal Wyoming. Slurring over Horn's unsavory
detective work and his hard-to-document activities during the Spanish-
American War, it mainly concerns his alleged murder of Willie
Nickell, aged fourteen, in southern Wyoming (July 1901), his subsequent arrest in Cheyenne (January 1902), his trial and conviction
there (October 1902), his abortive escape and reincarceration (August 1903), and his execution (November 1903).

Everything but a prefatory section entitled "The Beginning" and an afterword called "Beyond the Ending" purports to be Tom Horn's autobiographical deposition, miraculously preserved and tardily found. (Shades of *No Survivors, The Fourth Horseman, Who Rides with Wyatt, The Seven Men at Mimbres Springs, The Gates of the Mountains, Apache Ransom, Genesis Five* [to be treated later], and Thomas Berger's *Little Big Man.*) This deposition device results in startling directness and hence reader engagement, but with all that some awkwardness. On balance, *I, Tom Horn* is a stunning novel. As usual, Allen flips the coin to its less-studied reverse and makes a credible hero out of history's thug.

The novelist makes frequent drafts on Horn's own *Life of Tom Horn*, especially for his opening chapters, in which he creates a fresh Huck Finn-like young storyteller. Later, Allen fictionalizes considerably on Horn's Apache decade and gives him an Indian wife, sweet Nopal; avoids almost entirely Horn's activities as an Arizona deputy sheriff, rodeo cowboy, Pinkerton detective, Wyoming Cattleman's Association hit man, and civilian mule wrangler for the army;[19] and ingeniously has his hero, while stoically awaiting execution, both write this new manuscript, called *I, Tom Horn*, and also dream of a last-minute escape, reminiscent of Ambrose Bierce's "An Occurrence at Owl Creek Bridge," which Allen says he never read before he composed his novel.[20]

The novelist turns Horn into an autobiographer with a wild and salty sense of ribald humor which often borders on the obscene. The gunman also has a dark side and is aware that from his earliest years he has been warned by a shadow, or *Sombra*, as Spanish-speaking Horn calls it. Through not obeying its admonition to "Ride out, ride out," Tom succumbs to that unconscious, masochistic impulse which Edgar Allan Poe called "The Imp of the Perverse" and which makes some people rush to their own ruination. Carl Gustav Jung, to whom few Western writers listen, in all likelihood,[21] called this negative, often evil side of a person the Shadow. But Jung added that if a person is violent and bad, his Shadow may be a contrasting good; such is Tom Horn's *Sombra*, surely. Geronimo even reports that the gunman's son by Nopal is named " 'Sombra, after his father's shadow.' "[22]

In any event, Allen regards Horn as his own most dangerous enemy—wenching so much that one of his nicknames is "Wide Crotch" (143), drinking to excess and then becoming dangerously loose-tongued, daring and fighting, and also boasting—even lying—far too much. Rather early in his deposition Horn explains that "Lying was something I liked to do, and did it right well. Done proper, it could spare harm and bestow kindnesses, ease away pain and restore good feeling" (107). Later he bursts out with this: ". . . how banefully little true history tells of a man's real life as he himself knowed it and fought it out" (201). Close to the end he praises the honesty of his new defense attorney in this odd fashion: " 'Yes, he tells the truth. That's always trouble' " (313). Perhaps like tribal bards and the writers of epics, Tom Horn bends the truth into Truth. Without much doubt Allen believes that his hero was framed and may have so concluded ever since reading Eugene Cunningham's *Triggernometry,* in which the author back in 1934 effectively theorized as much.[23]

The seven novels discussed here fictionalize the lives of seven white gunmen. Two are real-life men whom Allen reviles. They are Jesse James, often idolized (though not in recent years), and Henry Plummer, always despised once exposed. Four are historical gun-fighters whom Allen probably treated more favorably than they deserve. They are Wyatt Earp, Butch Cassidy, Isom Dart, and Tom Horn. One character, a composite named Hush Feleen, is fictional and proves to be an enigmatic loner alternately touching and repellent. Interestingly, Allen lists among his dozen personal favorites, as we have seen, *The Raiders, Reckoning at Yankee Flat, One More River to Cross,* and *I, Tom Horn.* Perhaps he is disproportionately attracted to white gunmen in part wrongly treated by history and legend, and has sought to redress the record.

Chapter Six

Lust for Blood and Gold

In addition to fiction about Indians, horsemen, and gunmen good and bad, Henry Wilson Allen has produced novels about man's search for adventure and blood lust in war and also about man's search for gold, and the injustice and killing that result. Allen has been mainly concerned with the Civil War, writing three novels about it, but has also published one novel about the Spanish-American War. His life-long fascination with legends about lost gold mines has resulted in three novels; in addition, he has published one novel cast in Alaska during the Klondike rush. All eight of these novels also connect with the novelist's adoration of the West.

War

Allen subscribes to Herman Melville's famous poetic dictum that "All wars are boyish, and are fought by boys." So the central characters in his war novels are naturally enough mere kids—matured rapidly by gunfire, to be sure. As Melville also wrote, "What like a bullet can undeceive!" Since Allen's purpose seems to be to show the folly of war, it was appropriate perhaps that the novelist decided to make his Civil War combatants come from the South, specifically from Texas, so that their disillusionment could result from their participation in "the Lost Cause." This also could enable some of the works to connect with Indians, those other American participants in lost-cause military action. The psychological development of every Allen combat veteran is from illusion to cynicism, especially in his two best war novels, *The Crossing* and *Journey to Shiloh*.

The Crossing (1958). The historical background of *The Crossing* is as effectively managed as any in an Allen novel. It concerns the efforts of Confederate commanders Lieutenant Colonel John Robert Baylor and General Henry Hopkins Sibley to wrest the accurately depicted territory of New Mexico and Arizona from Union control, between June 1861 and May 1862. Familiar place names such as San Antonio, Fort Bliss, Fort Clark, Fort Fillmore, Mesilla, Fort Craig, Valverde, Albuquerque, Santa Fe, Fort Union, Apache Canyon, Glorietta, and the Rio Grande punctuate not only historical accounts of this region in the first years of the Civil War but also chapter after chapter of *The Crossing*.[1]

In it Judah Beaumont "Jud" Reeves, III, the nineteen-year-old Texas hero, is the son and grandson of brave generals. Like Button Starbuck of *The Blue Mustang*, Jud is gauche but resourceful, on the verge of manhood and destined to suffer a speedy maturation during combat. Like Johnny Ringo of *Who Walks with Wyatt*, Jud needs help from a surrogate father, or maybe two; but unlike Ringo, young Jud changes from naïve to humanely reliable. He joins Baylor as a scout and does creditably. Then he joins Sibley and soon sees enough sickening war to want out. Like most of Allen's heroes, Jud Reeves is thus pulled agonizingly in two directions. The poor lad tries hard to reflect credit upon his military family name and even faithfully carries into combat with him a monograph entitled *The Professional Soldier in Command: His Obligations as a Leader of Men*, written by his father, now dead. But the principal theme of *The Crossing*, like that of Melville's quite similar *Redburn*, is that books important to one generation are often no guide for the next, or rather that the ideals of one generation, as symbolized by the Reeves monograph, are often hurtful to the generation succeeding. Specifically, military leadership in *The Crossing* is dramatized as spelling death or injury to those who follow, or precede, their "leaders." Further, military honor here is spelled out as an empty word.

Jud undertakes to define war, before he has seen more than two brief bits of admittedly gory action, as "a pure crusade," in which dying is an honor and a patriotic service. On hearing this, a veteran scout named Elkanah Cavanaugh snorts at the youth and argues in favor of survival: "Dead men, he growled, did nothing for any country. It was the live ones who made the speeches over their graves and then went home to marry their widows and inherit their personal fortunes. The only service a man performed by dying for his side, was to shorten the war by just so much. The more killed, the sooner over. Jud would see."[2]

Jud does see. His most sickening moment comes when during the battle of Valverde (February 21, 1862) he shoots the face off a Union soldier with a 12-gauge shotgun. During the inexplicable retreat of the sick or drunk Sibley soon thereafter,[3] Jud has occasion to remember longest what Walt Whitman's immortal "Wound-Dresser" recalls with unique vividness too, that is, the wounds—or as Jud puts it, "the triple battleground specters of gangrene, tetanus and post-wound pneumonia" (240). Recovering from pneumonia himself, Jud meets his spiritual Rubicon—a titular crossing (Jud calls the Rio Grande his "Rubicon" [92])—when he decides to cross over a final time. He crosses from family to surrogate family, from army life to civilian life, from America to Apacheland, from mooncalf adoration of an unworthy white woman to the dusky arms of a half-breed girl. All this as he crosses physically from north of the Rio Grande down to the Mexican Sierra Madres for good. What he leaves behind is an unneeded, callow idealism. What he arrives at is a bracing, cynical realism. Young though he still is, he has earned his disillusioned mind-set.

The Crossing is balanced and exciting. In it Allen again blends the military and the amorous, this time by giving Jud's mentor Cavanaugh not only a Mexican-Apache wife but also a teen-aged daughter Estrellita (another "Star"). Jud loves her soon enough but takes a predictably long time choosing her over an insipid white woman named Felicia Horton. Sidetracking Jud is a partially idyllic though also harrowing vacation with an Apache band led by a good Indian and misled by an evil one. Though not told directly by Jud, the narrative filters through his juvenile consciousness. Sibley is yet another vacillating white officer. In short, *The Crossing* is commendable for its own merits but also reflects at least ten earlier Allen novels. As such, it makes an ideal introduction, somewhat as does the later *Chiricahua*, to the works of Allen, being in fact a kind of Allen anthology.

Journey to Shiloh (1960). *Journey to Shiloh* is a better war novel than *The Crossing*. It too avoids, though to a lesser degree, being simply another piece of romantic Civil War fiction. Although its seven central characters, all pathetically young Confederate volunteers, are Texas cowboys who "learned to ride at two, shoot at four, scalp at twelve, squaw at sixteen,"[4] Allen almost at once focuses on the hypocrisy and the hopelessness of the Old South's social, political, racist, and military position. So, like *The Crossing*, it is about more than war, although its more cramped canvas has no room for Indians and little for love.

Like most of Allen's fiction, *Journey to Shiloh* is tragicomic. It starts humorously, with a bunch of naïve lads rushing to join the

Confederate army in Richmond, which they never see, to fight the Yanks. They leave western Texas, gallop east past Dallas to Mendota, Shreveport, and then Vicksburg. On the train, they see some wild horses being mishandled by Confederate soldiers. Their offering to help results in their being dragooned into General Braxton Bragg's unit from Florida, the Light Blues; so they participate in the horrible action at Shiloh, are smashed, are more than decimated, and desert.

The point of view is that of seventeen-year-old Buck Burnett. The novel is in dissimilar halves. First it is largely fun, partly frustration, with lack of success gradually dominating. But the second half! It is ruinously bitter, disillusioned, tragic. Death punctuates the action like a runaway funeral bell. At Mendota the tiny amateur command attracts twin lads no older than themselves and as callow. The pair joins, but one injures a knee in a storm; infection and fever set in, then amputation, then death. This young veteran was a soldier six days. An original member of the group then loses his life in a Shreveport shootout. Buck aids a runaway slave at Munroe Station, only to turn him over to a lynch party, all unknowingly until he sees the truth too late. Near Corinth another of the intrepid seven dies, of pneumonia. During the climactic battle of Shiloh one is killed, then two more. Buck, the central boy-hero, witnesses the pathetic death of General Albert Sidney Johnston and then loses his left arm during Bragg's classic rearguard action to delay General U. S. Grant's pursuit of General P. G. T. Beauregard. The last lad of Buck's ragged command deserts, is dogged by Bragg's vicious military police, commits murder, and is killed. Glory, glory.

Journey to Shiloh is unified by the progressive disillusionment of its central characters. The last few chapters spiral down into an absolute nightmare. The unreal glare lighting most of the action is occasionally alleviated by gallows humor. A clever touch is Buck's not returning to one Gabrielle Marie Celeste Massanet, whom the lad encounters at Vicksburg and who threatens to become yet another soiled-dove heroine. Allen seems to say with Ernest Hemingway of *A Farewell to Arms* that a war-blasted land has no room for lasting love. Ultimately *Journey to Shiloh* is a pacifist document of considerable eloquence.

Summer of the Gun (1978).   Late in his career Allen again answered the challenge to fictionalize the effects of combat on Confederate soldiers, both pathetically young and also older this time. The result is *Summer of the Gun*, a novel of violence mixed with comedy.

In an opening that is somewhat detached from the main body Allen presents the background of the West Texas McAlister family homesteading at Paint Creek: back in 1858 the father Sunny Jim McAlister tried to track Sun Killer, a militant Comanche chief, for the Texas Rangers, but instead got his own head sent back in a sack to his wife Mary, as an honor to his fine tracking ability. Mary became demented. The boy hero, Bubba McAlister, was only eight but impressed Sun Killer as wild and tough enough to merit abducting and raising as a Comanche. But no kidnapping occurred. Three years pass, and the Civil War begins; Bubba's older brothers Lon and Junior prepare to join the rebel army, and do so after Sun Killer tries to take advantage of the war to snatch Bubba, only to be murderously repulsed. Bubba, his mother Mary, and his sister Sissy (aged thirteen but mature already) must now go to live in the seedy town of Red Hawk.

The Civil War is offstage in *Summer of the Gun* but is still monstrously influential. Lon writes home after Shiloh (why not a different battle from the one in *Journey to Shiloh?*): Lon has a ruined arm; Junior, a ruined leg. It takes them until June 1863 to be discharged and allowed to crawl back home to Texas (in chapter 9). In a sense, the forty-chapter novel only now begins.

Hearing that her soldier boys are coming, Mary enlists the help of Bubba, Sissy, and an old man named Cap Marston (once a Texas Ranger), and resumes residence at the old Paint Creek homestead. The scene shifts briefly to Fort Griffin, Shackleford County, Texas, on June 29, 1863, and to Lon and Junior there. The latter is now at death's door. The miserable pair are seized by eight assorted Confederate deserters led by a Gothic horror improbably named Captain Braxton Fragg (don't read Bragg), plus a heroic black named Scipio Africanus (Skip), and Gabby, an Indian mute. This weird gang includes depraved, homicidal sensualists. Inevitably, Allen puts them on an escape route through Paint Creek. The presence of old Mary and young Sissy makes the monsters positively drool. Meanwhile, since they have left a wake of robbery and murder, a tough old sheriff, name of Charley Skiles, and his reluctant posse are dogging the filthy trail of Fragg *et al.*

What transpires in the next two days comprises one of Allen's most grisly plots. The early promise of *Summer of the Gun* subsides into a pattern of rapes improbably deferred and juvenile derring-do too implausible to be taken seriously. The action becomes a sequence of false starts. Junior dies almost within sight of home. Skiles's posse quits on the trail, then starts again, but perilously late. Even his horse, named Kickapoo and possessed of a heroic personality, gets conveniently lost with all its gear intact, so that Bubba can happen upon needed weaponry. One after another death blows and near misses shake the plot like kettledrum notes. Allen directs his percussion section with versatility surpassing even his own previous efforts: tomahawk and knife, rifle and pistol, extra gunpowder up a carbine barrel, steel-jawed wolf trap, Molotov cocktail, wagon-wheel crushing. Mary fights back, biting a would-be assailant's ear off and finding herself mentally rejuvenated thereby, when unspeakable Fragg organizes a rape lottery for his squad's delectation.

San Juan Hill (1962).   This novel is unique in Allen's production. It has cowboys, yes. It has black troops, yes. It has fighting, yes. It has real-life characters, yes. But its main action occurs in Cuba, far from the geography and time-frame of the novelist's beloved Old West.

San Juan Hill is a curious novel, in four equal but somewhat unharmonized parts. The young Arizona cowboy hero, Fate Beylen, reads about the start of the war, quickly leaves home, and joins up, soon meeting a variety of soldier types (chapters 1-10). The unit, under Lieutenant Colonel Theodore Roosevelt, gets to Cuba and into preliminary action (chapters 11-20). Real-life Captain Buckey O'Neill[5] orders Fate to gather a posse and capture a disloyal, self-serving insurgent leader, which the hero does with the aid of a priest and a little girl (chapters 21-30). Then come the Battle of San Juan Hill, Fate's bravery thereat, his being wounded, and his farewell to arms and Roosevelt (chapters 31-40).

Unlike the youthful soldiers in *The Crossing, Journey to Shiloh,* and *Summer of the Gun,* young Fate of *San Juan Hill* does not become totally disillusioned and cynical. He does ridicule war as a pointless folly; but he also delights in the camaraderie of soldiers, and he does view Roosevelt as a man of destiny. In fact, Allen comes up with one of his most staggering puns when he has obedient Fate follow resolute Teddy.[6]

In addition to commenting on the futility of war, Allen in *San Juan Hill* contrasts Western cowboys and Eastern college football players, once they are thrown into action. For example, when horses, mules, and weapons go under water during the landing past Guantanamo Bay in Santiago Harbor, Cuba, the men slave to rescue what they can; but the difference is that the Arizona cowboys call it work while Eastern reporters call it heroism. To state matters reductively, the West is honest while the East is theatrical. Allen also suggests that historical accounts of events in the Spanish-American War are so incomplete and biased that there is really no truth, only different points of view, perspectives, and conclusions. Roosevelt is here not only the grand figure of "history" but also grinny, high-voiced; "go-as-you-please," histrionic, overmatched, defecting, prevaricating, and homicidally glory-seeking. (T. R. is here a little like Custer, though better toward his men; he was, however, lucky enough to survive and thus become president, precisely as Custer wished to do.) Allen ominously concludes at one point: "It would have historical significance for the Roosevelt dynasty, to be able to read the reports of one or two of the Arizona volunteers present during . . . what T. R. was later to call his 'trying fight' as Las Guásimas."[7] Allen takes pains to praise the black troops involved. A dramatic if gradual movement in the novel is the shift in key characters' minds from prejudice against blacks to confidence in them. Allen makes Buckey O'Neill put it all with unconscious humor and self-revelation: when Fate lauds Mexicans and voices trust, therefore, in Cubans too, O'Neill replies, " 'I would rather . . . put my own faith in one of Colonel Baldwin's Tenth Cavalry colored boys than to side with one of these damned [Cuban] insurgents. They are a shiftless lot . . . and would as soon knife one of us for our tobacco as not' " (135).

The final impression of *San Juan Hill* is that of a novel which combines great historical accuracy, thus depicting great bravery, and unacceptable derring-do which is no better, in actuality, than descriptions by Richard Harding Davis, who has a bit part in this work.

Four novels, then, of youth at war and the horrible consequences thereof. Heroism, yes, but with it fate's spendthrift pouring out of rich young blood. The abiding effects are disillusionment at least, and at worst cynicism forced into expression too soon, from the mouths of maimed babes in arms.

Gold

As potent as lust for blood in war is lust for gold in the ground. Hence four Allen novels about man's insane and violent scramble for gold. *The North Star* is unique, through being cast in Alaska. Three other stories take us much farther south, to Allen's familiar Apa-

cheria. They are *Mackenna's Gold*, his best gold novel; *Tayopa!*,
unusual through taking place in the late 1960s; and *Black Apache*,
which is a sequel to *Apache Ransom*, discussed in Chapter 3.

The North Star (1956).   This novel, like *San Juan Hill*, and
See How They Run and *Genesis Five* (both to be considered later),
is cast in a region Allen never visited. All the same, Alaskan cold
is described so well that parts of the book were surely written with
the same icicle that Melville said Richard Henry Dana, Jr., must
have used when he described rounding Cape Horn in *Two Years
Before the Mast.*

One of its most delightful features is our discovery that the hero
Murrah Starr, a half-breed loner with a hidden gold mine, is the son
of Cetan Mani and his wife Star of the North (of *No Survivors*).
Young Starr never saw his father, was adopted by Sitting Bull, and
was educated in a white school in Dakota. He escaped from it with
an Indian friend, later killed by soldiers in a border clash which
gave Starr a bullet-crippled leg. On his way to Canada he came upon
a trapped wolf, freed him, named him Sotaju (Sioux for "Smoke"),[8]
and was loved forever by the ferocious beast. Starr then worked for
a good white trapper named Murray (hence Starr's first name), whose
murder by a poacher caused ignorant Canadian Mounties to push
Starr west, all the way to Nome, Alaska. All of this is background,
revealed in a reminiscence by Starr to the heroine, beautiful Erin
Eileen O'Farrell, a Russian priest's teen-aged housekeeper in Nome.

The fast-paced novel falls into tidy quarters. Starr comes to Nome
for supplies, but gets into a fight and is almost killed by a gang of
whites led by villainous Black Angus McClennon (whose dog Smoke
casually tears apart when challenged). The whites want to learn the
location of Starr's secret mine, called the North Star, in the subarctic
interior. Starr is dragged to safety by Erin and cared for, then returns to
his cabin, and kills a couple of pursuing attackers but avoids several
others (chapters 1-7).

While his enemies file on his claim, now located, and organize a
party to lynch the "murderer," Starr returns to Erin for new supplies,
tells her about himself and is repulsed after he mistakes her sympathy
for passion, makes his way back to his shack, dynamites some of his
remaining enemies who are in it, but is temporarily blinded in the
process and is tracked by still more pursuers (chapters 8-14).

Now *The North Star* shifts its point of view cinematically from

Erin, assembling aid for Starr, to the hero himself, whom faithful Smoke leads into a cave providing an uncertain sanctuary (chapters 15-19).

Starr, when he can see again, escapes only to fall into a freezing stream, and must amputate his own frozen and log-dead leg to stay ahead of the "posse." Not only continuing danger from McClennon and his gang but also the ultimate salvation which Erin and a stalwart Finn with a fresh dog team could provide are now zeroing in on the indomitable hero. An incredible but stirring climax rings the curtain down (chapters 20-26).

Several aspects of this novel are noteworthy. The plot becomes psychologically complex after Erin deters Starr's wolfish advances by calling him a half-breed (". . . the vicious lash of the word cut into Murrah Starr like a dog whip").[9] Starr is epically heroic in his refusal to say die. Allen depicts the −60° Alaskan wasteland matchlessly. Best of all, he symbolically equates Starr and his wolf Smoke: each is lonely, crippled, vicious, loyal, and admirable; further, like a good wolf, Starr mates for life! The half-breed's success in winning pale Erin is a welcome reversal of the outcome of *Red Blizzard*.

Mackenna's Gold (1963). In an Author's Note Allen acknowledged J. Frank Dobie's *Apache Gold & Yaqui Silver* as the nonfictional inspiration of *Mackenna's Gold*. Dobie's 1939 book must have haunted the novelist, first because he uses many details of its chapter called "The Lost Adams Diggings" in *Mackenna's Gold* (especially chapters 25 and 26), second because Dobie's "The Lost Tayopa Mine" chapter led him to write *Tayopa!*, and third because Dobie's "El Naranjal" chapter is the foundation of the last part of Allen's *Black Apache*.[10]

Mackenna's Gold connects not only with Dobie but also with several of Allen's other works. Thus Pelón, the Chihuahua renegade villain of the novel, is said to have been with the Apache Kid three years earlier, back in 1894 during the Kid's last raid. Another unsavory fellow in *Mackenna's Gold* is Hachita, grand-nephew of Mangas Coloradas. At one point the hero Glen Mackenna sends for reinforcements to Al Sieber, but that sensible survivor declines the siren call of Apache gold. Showing up instead is young Mickey Tibbs, fictional son of real-life Mickey Free, a scout friend of Tom Horn. Accompanying the gold seekers is a murderous Apache beauty prosaically called Sally; she is Pelón's half-sister, takes a revealing nude swim to entice timorous Mackenna, but instead arouses Hachita, the wrong man for her. Allen devotees will detect echoes of his earlier works.

In the same key, too, is awesome violence in *Mackenna's Gold*. The villain slugs the hero, breaking one of his teeth; later he chips the hero's collarbone with his revolver barrel, by way of warning him to stop talking to lovely white captive Francie Stanton, with whom the hero too suddenly realizes he is in love. Next, the villain slits the hero's chest twenty inches, but thinly, to emphasize another conversational point. When a cohort voices homesickness, the villain calls out "hello," shoots him in the stomach, then crushes his head with a stone; the chapter in which this action occurs is called "Good-bye in the Belly."[11] Yet another comrade tactlessly tells the villain to go to hell, whereupon " '*Despues de Usted*,' he murmured politely, 'after you' " (82), and squeezes off a fatal shot from his serape-hidden Colt. A cavalry ambush depletes the villain's band. Oversexed Sally endures an amorous embrace so macho that it breaks her neck. Mickey murders two black troops. Ever humorous, the villain when axed deep in the chest confesses that, sure enough, he does not have a soft spot after all, which the hero half doubted. Mickey's demise is accomplished by a combination of bullet in knee, to slow him down, and hatchet in mouth. Even Francie figures in the mayhem: while the hero blinds Hachita with dust, then groin-kicks him, she brains him with a handy axe.

These echoes and gorinesses should not mislead the reader. *Mackenna's Gold* is a brilliant work of fiction. It falls into seven-chapter sixths. Its themes are greed and the distinction between appearance and reality. The story dramatizes the nature of evil: Pelón is pure villainy, a killer with a wolf-grin. Lust for gold almost turns Mackenna and Francie ruinously bad. If they had stayed to violate the resting place of the gold, the God-sent earthquake would have destroyed them even as it beautifully reburies the Apache treasure. Thus *Mackenna's Gold* becomes a Chaucerian, Travenesque parable,[12] the moral of which is surely "Give the gold back to the earth, and so to legend." The ghostly ending of the novel is one of Allen's best. The survivors of the earthquake receive a message from a dead Chiricahua Apache, thanking them for sparing his sacred land from desecration. What I remember longest, however, is not that but a haunting description of smells in Apacheria:

It was a lovely night. The desert smelled as only the desert can smell after an enormously hot day. The sun's heat had baked out of each stone and grain of sand and tiny arid-leaved plant its entire fragrance. Now, with several hours of cooling darkness to soften them, these earthen odors and these pungent scents of sage, beargrass, prickly pear and Spanish dagger were rising to meet the nose in a delight of horse-stirred dust, sweated saddle leather and acrid, biting tang of pony droppings. It was the sort of wanderer's wind which men of Mackenna's ... lone breed drank heavily. (96)

Tayopa! (1970).   Allen's first novel in a contemporary setting is *Tayopa!*, which he published under his own name. About the legendary Sonora gold mine, the book is really a western which forgot to stay in its proper century. In some ways its locale is outside normal time. Its main character, the one who occasions all the action, is Pancho Gaona, appropriately nicknamed El Niño Perdido. He seems to be a little boy: apparently eight or ten years old, he really goes back three centuries in terms of experience, knowledge, wisdom, and the smarts to guard the fabulous Tayopa treasure from outsiders and would-be desecrators. This Nuhuatlan Indian kid collects quarters of a map which, when assembled, can show the location of the treasure mine to a congeries of adult fools whom Pancho alternately aids and frustrates.

Like *Chiricahua* and *The Bear Paw Horses, Tayopa!* is full of bewildering action. The closest thing to it in recent movies is the 1981 *Raiders of the Lost Ark*. The lost gold lures seven adults—count them—or, to be more exact, seven adults or sets of adults. One is Father Bernalillo Díaz, a spoiled priest whose name is designed to evoke memories of earlier Spanish despoilers of lower Apacheria.[13] Father Díaz superficially resembles Father Panfilo Alvar Nunez, the likable *Apache Ransom* priest whom we will meet again in *Black Apache.* But Díaz becomes so depraved that he seems to be a reincarnation of a certain evil Jesuit from seventeenth-century Mexico.[14] Next are a corrupt Mexican guide named D. Jaime Guzmán and his tourist customers—Mari C. Schultzmann, who is willowy and blonde, and talks dirty a lot (her favorite word seems to be "shit"),[15] and her gentler friend Lisa Louise "Lissy" Farrasey. They are comely California schoolteachers on a Sonora summer fling. Next we meet little Pancho and his wiry grandfather, Garibaldi Gaona; the old rascal is eighty, is a retired panther hunter, and has prostate trouble. The heroic anti-hero

of *Tayopa!* is Joe Lobo (Josef Kosciuski Loboski for long). He is
more wicked than even Hush Feleen; a major coup of the novel is
the way in which Allen makes us give Joe our grudging sympathy.
You see, Joe is an American heroin smuggler, a murderer, a bush
pilot, and an awful male chauvinist wolf with an eye on Lissy's "great
tits and . . . class ass" (149). Opposing Joe is a depraved, grinning
gang of Mafia hit men down from north of the border on orders to
rub out Joe for defecting. Allen provides this group with colorful
names. The leader is Guiseppe "Blinky" Salerno, and his two hench-
men are Benjamin Franklin Eichman ("Bennie the Eyeball" for
short) and Albert "Bones" Caligulari. They smack more of Keystone
cops than *Godfather*. To Father Díaz, Guzmán and party, the Gaonas,
and the Syndicate gunnies and their wary quarry, add two more
squads. They are stolid, honorable Sergeant Cheno Cruz, his Pima
guide Paco X. Reyes, and their Mexican Rurale army unit, all afoot,
and vicious Captain Hektor Morales and Sergeant Garcia, who comprise a pro-government Mexican Federale army unit, mostly aloft
in a helicopter.

How can Allen manage such a diversity of characters in one story
which any sane reader can keep straight and even make sense out of?
Remember *Iktomi*, the tiny spidermen who the Sioux say weave webs
of sorrow trapping men and tumbling them together with an ever-
faster motion? Those spidermen from *The Bear Paw Horses*? Well,
Allen calls upon an almost identical image in *Tayopa!* when he
notes that "[t]he spider spins her web toward the center, even if
working outward all the while. And when the plan is completed,
its victims, whether of pure chance or the spinner's design, caught
alike on outer or inner strands, are drawn toward the common center,
none the less, where all are welcomed and each awaited by the arach-
nid weaver of their tangled fates" (126). Later, when Lisa and Joe
have fallen in love, Allen returns to the spider figure: "Perhaps
neither [of the lovers] warped the spider's web, or hastened, by a
single silk-spun thread, the pattern's shrinking funnel. . . . No matter.
The weaver does not know, she simply weaves . . ." (190). Likewise,
Allen the master storyteller seems less to "know" than merely to
tangle his web and let his characters be thus drawn by many modes
of travel to the center, which is the Tayopa treasure site, near
Nàcori, in north-central Sonora.[16] The spider web catches one character after another—a couple of dozen in all—killing no fewer than
fourteen.

As if to prove that fatal spiders have operated in all centuries, Allen cast *Tayopa!* in our century. But without changing any essential details, we could move this novel back one century—to the late 1860s. The golden legend would then be only a couple of hundred years old. So would jade-eyed little Pancho. The mad Santa Clara priest with his jeep could have traveled down instead from any California mission on a mule. The mobsters might easily have been displaced Civil War veterans, perhaps like Braxton Fragg and his homicidal troops, from *Summer of the Gun*. Nuhuatlan eyesight would have more than compensated for any view through helicopter binoculars. Then no one would have doubted that Allen's first contemporary novel was yet another gory western.

A timeless element which punctuates most of the narrative divisions of this long novel is the changing relationship of Joe and Lisa. When they first meet, they argue and he throws her off her feet. But soon he enjoys the sight of Lisa and her dirty-mouthed friend when the Rurales order them to undress and be searched. Later Joe and Lisa have a nude swim together; but just as they are about to improve their beach time, little Pancho dives in to interrupt, and we read of Joe's "[t]umescent manhood wilting as some shyest adolescent" and then the man drops into the water "like a ruptured submarine" (121). Yet again the enflamed pair are frustrated—this time by the pop-chuff of Morales's helicopter pancaking down to have a look. The description is comic-erotic beyond belief, and all the more grotesque in that only moments earlier they disposed of three Syndicate corpses. But at last, treasure near and Tayopa's mystic bells whispering encouragement on the wind, Joe Lobo and Lisa Farrasey consummate their Neanderthal passion and learn what Allen often records: mating is "the rarest wealth in God's gift" (190). This is the true treasure of Tayopa. The two, among others, sought gold, but found love and death.

Another moral of this novel is that it never pays to insult old things, especially old men, old legends, or little boys like Pancho Gaona, who may seem callow but who is really 322 years old—and immortal, or at least appears so until his gold is safe again.

Recall that an earthquake buried Mackenna's gold. Tayopa's treasure is safely submerged under flood waters. What happens to the lost fortune of El Naranjal? Read on.

Black Apache (1976).   The least effective of the four gold-mine novels is *Black Apache*. It is a sequel to *Apache Ransom* but has a plot that is more melodramatic and superficial. *Black Apache* raids a number of Allen's previous novels. Thus Father Nunez, Flicker,[17] Kaytennae, and Kifer are from *Apache Ransom*. Stella Allison, sister of redoubtable Ben (of *The Tall Men, The Big Pasture, The Return of the Tall Man*, and *Apache Ransom*), appears briefly in *Black Apache*. Packrat from *The Apache Kid* volunteers to join the Naranjal expedition. We go up to Tombstone, locale of *Who Rides with Wyatt*, and figuring slightly in both *The Fourth Horseman* and *I, Tom Horn*. Tom Horn is discussed in *Black Apache* as "Tin Horn"[18] but does not appear. Shieffelin Ledge, from *I, Tom Horn*, is also mentioned. And there are echoes from *Mackenna's Gold* and *Tayopa!*

One of the best features of *Black Apache* is its occasionally haunting prose style, which reads a bit like a translation from a quaint old Spanish text, reminiscent of Thornton Wilder's *The Bridge of San Luis Rey*.[19] This is the effect Allen sought, since here again we have what purports to be a recovered document—the journal of Panfilo Nunez, O.F.M., 1879. Allen explains that he has translated everything and even notes that his Apache-language passages differ from those of standard phonetic texts.

Black Apache is an outrageous combination of history, fabrication parading as history, brutal realism, weird plot twists and coincidences which we are asked to accept because they answer Father Nunez's prayers for divine aid—who can quarrel with God's will?—and fantasy mounting to the level of legend.

The action concerns the efforts of Father Nunez to dart north of the U.S.-Mexican border into the Tombstone area to recruit help in following a miraculously provided map back down into Mexico and then in engineering the hidden gold out again. This not for Nunez or anyone else personally, but to angel his establishing an unpreachy church for Apaches. The gang which he assembles include Flicker, Kaytennae, Packrat, a pair of ultra-bosomy females named Zorra and Charra, and a tough trail dog. And there are others. Meanwhile, still others seek to prevent or to anticipate the gold lift. They include villainous Kifer, his depraved Apache mother Monkey Woman and her disgustingly atavistic other son, a small horde of subhuman Yaquis, and—best of all—a little corps of ghostly Tepehuana guards from the lost mines of long ago.

What the reader remembers of the plot of *Black Apache* is that he cannot remember it. It is an impossible tangle, but fun. Unity comes as Nunez and Flicker, thrown together again by the hand of God, gradually experience a meeting of minds and souls. Nunez may be misshapen—only five feet tall, nicknamed *Jorobado* (Hunchback, Broken Back), and Rat Turd—but he is indomitable. Flicker is even more glossy and supple than he was in *Apache Ransom*: stalking the Yaquis who have hurt Stella Allison, he is nothing less than a killer lion. But under the tutelage and example of Nunez, Flicker accepts spiritual values, albeit with a growl. Unity is also provided through a sustained high melody of harmless scatology—"noble mammaries" (100), urine, feces, "gonadal ambition" (8), and the like. An occasional lapsing of Allen's prose rhythm into incantatory iambs becomes predictable, too, and charming.

The lost gold of Naranjal, like Mackenna's and that of Tayopa, remains lost. Instead of being buried by earthquake or flood, though, the gold near the River of the Oranges, down Naranjal way, simply dissolves from the vision of its entranced beholders. Or did they ever really see it? After all, momentary sight of the mine is said "to steal the breath, to isolate the mind in warp of time and space beyond human imagining" (190). Under such circumstances, many questions properly remain unanswered in this latest fairy tale by Henry Allen, whose moral here once again is that God's most precious gift to us is not gold but love.

Allen's eight novels about blood lust in war and greed for gold combine to sermonize, in spite of bellowing plots, that peace is better than either victory or defeat, and that love of man for woman, woman for man, and both for nature and God is better than any other riches.

Chapter Seven

Miscellaneous Fiction and Criticism

Allen has proved anew his already demonstrated versatility by publishing about fifty short stories in various popular Western magazines (and then reprinting the best three dozen or so in book form), five superb books for children, two other novels which are hard to categorize (one is a contemporary criminal thriller, and the other a wild science-fiction job), and a few fugitive essays which may be called literary criticism.

Short Stories

Allen's short stories should be discussed next because they are closest in content and tone to the novels already treated. In fact, as we shall see, a few of them are rewrites of episodes from some of those novels. Of his stories, he writes "[m]y approach to short fiction is a bit different than most. More irony, humor, audacity and, always, romanticism. That's as vehemently opposed to romance" (A to G, 6/4/80).

Allen's best stories are all cast in the West and concern, half and half, Indian-white clashes and all-white clashes. It might be possible to treat them in a sequence similar to the one that I used in discussing the novels; but since they lack the versatility of his long fiction, I should like instead to discuss the stories in the order in which they were reprinted in book form.

The Oldest Maiden Lady in New Mexico and Other Stories (1962). This first short-story collection by Allen displays commendable variety. One tale is straight comic ("The Oldest Maiden Lady in New Mexico"); three are historomantic ("King Fisher's Road," "The Hunting of Tom Horn," and "A Mighty Big Bandit"); four, white fictional ("The Redeeming of Fate Rachel," "Sundown Smith," "The Deputization of Walter Mendenhall," and "The Trap");

two, Indian-white dramatic ("Pretty Face" and "The Chugwater Run"); and two, fable-like ("Isley's Stranger" and "Ghost Town").

"The Oldest Maiden Lady in New Mexico" (alternate title: "Able John") is raucously comic, like *The Day Fort Larking Fell*, although the characters are virtually all white and the story is all fiction. One might think from the title that the heroine would be immemorially old. A retired madam perhaps? An oft-consulted seeress? A matriarch full of memories of the really Old West? Not so. Humorously, she is but twenty-three, though feeling her celibate years. When an itinerant preacher-teacher named Able John Arkwright, partly patterned on Washington Irving's Ichabod Crane, comes to Eagle Nest, in New Mexico Territory, Abbie Kate Louise Gresham sets her cap for him, engaged though she is to "the local Brom Bones,"[1] one Cleburne "Clebe" McSween, whom our latter-day Ichabod discommodes—with a slingshot. Suspenseful, mock-epical, long-winded, this story is a delight.

"King Fisher's Road" owes its inspiration to the most famous incident in Texas outlaw-lawman John King Fisher's short but checkered career: his appropriating the public road to his ranch by planting in the exact middle of that road a sign attesting to his ownership of it and advising strangers to "take the other" (118). In this short story Allen has his narrator, an official road-opener for the American Mail company, rid the route of its obstacle by accepting deadly Fisher's challenge. Since the narrator can choose the weapons, he wins—with fists, not Colts—then deputizes the outlaw. No more trouble, for a while. The story is a bit contrived and inconsequential.

"The Redeeming of Fate Rachel" has an elaborate plot. An aging bounty hunter, Fate Rachel, ruthlessly kills a murderer whom he sent to prison ten years earlier but who, when released, is so foolish as to come gunning for him. This time Fate redeems himself by giving the reward money to the murderer's abandoned wife and needy daughter. Allen enriches what might have been some rather routine pulp fiction with oneiric overtones: Fate's second encounter with the gunman dreamily replicates the first and features a pause in which "the seconds of silence [are] like drops of life's blood" (97).

"Pretty Face" has for hero a mountain man named Hurd Clinton and for ultimately treasured heroine a Hunkpapa Sioux girl named Wastewin (Pretty Face). She agrees to trap him into desiring a roll in the grass by a grove so that her Indian cohorts can jump him and take his valuable sable and mink peltries. But she becomes so responsive to his roving hands that she defects. The consequence is torture, escape, love, and a clever climax in which the real villain gets his comeuppance offstage.

"The Chugwater Run" is the most history-oriented story in the collection. It pits He Dog, ally of unseen Red Cloud, American Horse, and Crazy Horse, against a green young Chugwater & Cheyenne stagecoach employee named Johnny D. He Dog and Johnny meet between fictitious Fort C. S. Shifter (i.e., Fort C. F. Smith) and Fort Phil Harny (Fort Phil Kearny) in momentous July 1866, during the buildup on both Indian and army sides before the Fetterman massacre. Relating to both *Red Blizzard* and *Warbonnet*—one for historical background and the other for the booming climax—"The Chugwater Run" is noteworthy for action enough to fill a novella, ghastly viciousness, myth elements, and a touch of romance.

"Sundown Smith" likewise has violence, but with it memorable evocations of lovely nature and quiet natural goodness, as old drifter Sundown Smith finds himself mistaken for a brutal killer and must save not only the beast's next young victim but also himself. This morality play pits the good and the natural against man-caused evil, and offers a Western-code ending uniquely scary in Allen.

"The Hunting of Tom Horn" starts with the narrator, a cattle-association detective named Charlie Shonto, rescuing Tom Horn from a lynching party somewhere between Lordsburg and Tucson, much the way Hush Feleen will do in the later novel *The Feleen Brand.* Horn then turns on Shonto but subsequently acts so heroically that the latter can hardly object. Richly plotted, partly comic in tone—Horn has "a grin crackly enough to warm your hands by on a cold day" (215)—and bristling with verisimilitude, "The Hunting of Tom Horn" must have made its first readers hope that Allen would return to Horn, which he did with *I, Tom Horn.*

"A Mighty Big Bandit" sentimentalizes Cole Younger shamelessly, dramatizing a fictitious event in the life of Jesse James's reluctant partner. Cole is here made to pause during his escape from deadly Northfield, Minnesota, to save a sweet little girl from murderous Charlie Pitts, another member of the riddled gang. With great ingenuity Allen weaves this fiction back into the story of Pitts's real-life death. The narrator, a vacationing Pinkerton who happens upon the action, complains that "[b]eing a detective for twenty years warps a man's morals" (218). Allen's devotion to Western American history never warped his fictive imagination.[2]

"Isley's Stranger," Allen's finest short story, concerns a man named Eben, a stranger who enters the tale on a mule and who is as magical as the Christ of the Apocrypha. He helps Tom Isley, a wandering cowboy, to arrange peace without bloodshed between feuding cattle- men and sheepmen in northwestern Wyoming out beyond Wolf Mountain flats. Eben is seen only intermittently by people other than Tom. And Tom himself, after the miracle is consummated, would doubt his own vision but for Eben's leaving him a copy of the *Rubaiyat* before vanishing. Earlier, Eben sermonizes with intense power: " 'Neither side ever wins a war. The best that can be done is that some good comes out of the bad; that, in some small way, the rights of the innocent survive. . . . [The meek] never inherit anything but the sins of the strong, unless they have help in time' " (247).

"The Deputization of Walter Mendenhall" (alternate title: "The Bad Samaritan") has red herrings, is paced with multiple climaxes, but is very clever at the end. In it a traveling shoe-salesman named Walter Mendenhall is deputized by the sheriff of Eudora, Wyoming, to help track and catch a resourceful bank robber and alleged killer. He is Curly Purcell. The posse runs him down, ties him up, posts a guard, and sacks out for the night. Taking his turn as guard, Walter is softsoaped by the criminal into letting him go—only to get slugged. Walter is forgiven, returns to town, finds half the loot in his inside pocket, uneasily decides to clam up, disposes of his shoe samples, and leaves by lonely stagecoach. Only to be held up. Curly strikes again. False clues make the unwary reader wonder if the local sheriff was criminally inclined, if Curly was his aide, if the whole town connived to con the Eastern greenhorn. It pays to read Allen's am- biguities subtly—and it is fun, too.

"Ghost Town" is beautifully subtle. A little boy breaks away from a bunch of tourists, some of whom see the old whilom mining town as rather like a rotting movie set, a mere trap for the callow. But the kid talks to nothing less than the reincarnation of the town's original settler. The two walk away and sit "on a sunny bench of sandstone which looked out over the Pahquoc Valley" (301), between the Cortege Mountains and the Bay Rum Hills this side of the Santilla Range. The codger narrates the life and death of the wilder- ness area, made fertile by his discovery of a secret underground river but then ruined by gold miners with their infernal dynamite. The little boy accepts this vision from the old man's shade of what that garden spot of the Old West was like back in the 1850s. I look upon this gentle story in two ways. First, it is Allen's fable of his West a century back. But second, it is also Allen's hint to us that his creative spirit can evoke that past in the minds and hearts of imaginative readers, if they care enough.

"The Trap" is an eldritch work. In it a cowboy, who robbed a bank and reluctantly killed a teller, is now being pushed relentlessly by a vigorous posse. Then his horse breaks a leg and must be shot. Why not let the beast suffer? Because it just isn't done in the West. But the revolver's roar tells the posse exactly where the outlaw is. Reality now blends into fantasy, as the topography begins to unroll before the doomed man exactly as he imagines it should; he even sees mustang tracks, then a mustang. Mounting, riding, and leaping to a spot on the box canyon's far wall, this Bierce-like figure is carried in thought beyond his own death. His terminal leap was only mental.

Most of these dozen stories are first-rate. They run the tonal gamut. Realism vies with the romantic and the oneiric. What I mainly take from them is a renewed respect for Allen's range, and also the impression that Allen loves not only history in its more violent stages but its chortles and shivers as well.

The Last Warpath (1966).   This book is one of Allen's most baffling. Composed of eight chapters—separate in time, setting, and action—it still has the unity of, say, William Faulkner's *Go Down, Moses*, Shelby Foote's *Jordan County*, or James Michener's *Hawaii*. *The Last Warpath* adumbrates, in miniature and by vignettes, the history of the Cheyenne Indians. Some of the segments are straight fiction, but mostly they are representative fictionalized history pieces. Each is a unit, but the units spread and coalesce into an aesthetic whole.

"The Pale Eyes" shadows forth the Cheyennes from 1680 to the mid-1850s. The first pale eyes that the Chahi-yena see are French explorers and fort builders in Canada. Goodfeather's grandmother relates old legends to the girl, whose son Lame Bear has a daughter named Lighting Swan. Then Assiniboins bring death to the Cheyenne people. Old at forty, Lighting Swan marries Far Hills Elk, has a son, Whistling Elk, who sees the Mandans, and Lewis and Clark, in 1804. In fear of the encroaching whites many Cheyennes become elusive and kite-like in their dipping over the horizon. Time goes on, to the 1830s, which usher in the white man's whiskey and Oregon Trail; then to the 1850s, and smallpox, cholera, and death in many other forms. The piece is less a story than a summary, and less that than a prose poem.

"Little Dried River" retells the horrors of Chivington, Black Kettle, and the Sand Creek massacre—from the pro-Indian point of view of Jack Smith, half-breed son of Uncle John Smith and his Indian squaw. Jack hears the Governor of Colorado promise immunity to Black Kettle but then sees Chivington's subsequent depravities. Fascinating details of Indian life figure in this work, which, however, suffers through repeating much action already published in *The Squaw Killers*.[3]

"Half-Blood Brother" is also repetitious. In it, Allen retells the first part of *Yellow Hair*, with Joshua Kelso renamed Blunt. Both are Custer's scouts. Whereas Kelso loved Monaseetah, Black Kettle's interpreter, Blunt wants Moheya (Blue Sky), Black Kettle's interpreter here. The earlier maiden was affianced to Mad Wolf; the later, to Death Horn Bull. Each violent suitor has two violent fellow warriors (Yellow Buffalo and Big Body of *Yellow Hair* become Yellow Cat and Fat Bear) to complicate the fighting which sweeps up each hero. Custer's horses get run off again. Custer's brother Tom reappears here. But the curious climax of "Half-Blood Brother" varies from that of the earlier novel: Blunt declines Moheya and rides off alone—perhaps because of his half-blood status. It may well be true that, as Blunt puts it, " 'No man should be born half-white and half-red. It's a bad color.' "[4]

"Red Runs the Washita" redacts the military parts of *Yellow Hair*, that is, Custer's attack on Black Kettle's Washita camp. Now Kelso becomes one Micah Carmody; Black Kettle, Bright Hair, and the squad of named army scouts remain the same; Joel Elliott dies again; Mad Wolf, Big Body, and Yellow Buffalo reappear; and so on.

"Peace of the Pony Soldiers" next retells the story of Colonel Reynolds's misguided attack on Cheyenne chief Two Moons and that redoubtable Sioux leader He Dog (from "The Chugwater Run"). Both of these Indian leaders in January 1876 had almost joined forces with hold-out Crazy Horse. Allen handled all of this—including Grabber's villainy and General Crook's disgust with Reynolds—in *No Survivors*. In "Peace of the Pony Soldiers," however, it is not Cetan Mani and Yellow Bird who warn the Indians, but a brave young Indian named Tonkalla. Now, Tonkalla (Mouse) is the Oglala Sioux hero, grown up and tough here, of Allen's book for children entitled *Valley of the Bear* (to be considered later). His being dis-

patched by Crazy Horse to aid the Cheyennes is a demonstration of
the necessity for cooperation between disputatious Indian tribes. Real-
life military details in "Peace of the Pony Soldiers," obviously an
ironic title, are substantially as in *No Survivors*. Again, Crazy Horse
is highly praised: when he rises in council, he is acknowledged by
"the guttural *'hun-hun-he!'* admiration growl reserved for the greatest
heroes only"; Allen adds in an authorial aside that "Crazy Horse was,
by common consent of the army commanders who met him in the
field, the greatest natural cavalry leader of modern times" (161).
By contrast, Sitting Bull is thoroughly presented here as "the law-
maker" (158) to whom Tonkalla brings news. This sketch is exciting,
but its main value lies less in its being well-dramatized fiction than
summary history from the Indian point of view.

"Way of the War Chief" is a retelling of the first part of *The Brass
Command*; that is, it presents again the escape of Little Wolf, the
Cheyenne war chief, and his pacifist associate Dull Knife from Oklahoma toward Fort Robinson. The action breaks off at the point when,
after the chiefs agree to separate, Dull Knife's grandson Red Bird
volunteers to join Little Wolf on his way west to freedom, rather
than go to the fort and passivity. Little Wolf will not let the young
teen-ager do so; instead, he dramatically gives him his own engraved
Winchester rifle with the order that the boy remain with his grandfather. Details of this episode, Allen concludes, are "still repeated with
tribal pride upon the Montana and Wyoming reservations" (192).

"Maheo's Children," its title reused for Allen's novel *Maheo's
Children*, later renamed *The Squaw Killers,* continues the ransacking
of *The Brass Command*, telling as the story does the last part of the
novel. "Maheo's Children" starts with Dull Knife and his 150 followers locked in the Fort Robinson barracks. Major Weston (here much
simplified) and Captain Jackson (nicknamed Black Hair) are in
charge. Once the honest pleas of the Cheyennes for peace are dis-
honorably ignored, they plan their almost suicidal breakout. The self-
sacrificial rearguard volunteers are positioned. Then everything follows
as in G. B. Grinnell's *The Fighting Cheyennes*—and *The Brass Command*. Even Sergeant John Henry Lundy (Jack here) reappears,
although, to keep the story plot simple, he is not sexually involved
with any homesteading farmer's widow, as in the novel. And the
moral of the action is stated more explicitly than in *The Brass Command*: in failing, both Weston and the Cheyenne leaders found
"[p]ride and freedom" (233).

"The Last Warpath," the eighth and last segment of the book called *The Last Warpath*, is the finest piece in it. Here Allen moves us onward to 1896. The scene is Wounded Knee, six years after the massacre. We enter the consciousness of an old Cheyenne, Spotted Wolf. Brought here by his gnarled daughter, Moheya, survivor of both Sand Creek and the Washita, and the unwed beloved of "Half-Blood Brother" Blunt, Spotted Wolf reminisces feebly about events leading to the Wounded Knee debacle. Cheyenne trackers aided the army in locating Sioux chief Big Foot, who was subsequently killed right here. Little Wolf was there and later relayed details to Spotted Wolf, saying that in death Big Foot seemed to be holding out his arms and expressing his conviction that, when the Cheyennes killed off the Sioux, they also killed themselves. Moheya understands and then turns to her father Spotted Wolf. But his hands are cold now, and he is dead.

Who was old Spotted Wolf? The son of Whistling Elk, whose story we should recall from "The Pale Eyes," the first piece in *The Last Warpath*, which thus began with an account of Moheya's great-great-great-grandmother Goodfeather.[5]

Read by one familiar with previous Allen novels, *The Last Warpath* is disappointing. But if one approaches it innocent of such antecedents, the book is both captivating as fiction and enlightening historically.

Red Brother and White (1966). In 1966 Allen published a two-volume collection of short stories called *Sons of the Western Frontier*. The first volume, *Red Brother and White*, contains five tales about very young heroes either red of skin or white, mostly clashing with their racial opposites. Unfortunately, four of the five plots derive from previous Allen novels. The second volume is called *Outlaws and Legends*, with six stories, again for the most part starring brave youths. Four of the stories are happily original; but the other two are, once again, rewrites.

"The Friendship of Red Fox" tells of the heroism of ten-year-old Red Fox, who, during a killing spree instigated by some Sioux from the northwestern Nebraska Pine Ridge agency, leads a woman, just widowed by those Indians, and her three children to safety within the confines of a distant army fort. Allen's depiction of murderous braves is counterbalanced by one vicious anti-white statement: it seems that the boy hero's Indian relatives thought he "ought to be taught the white man's ways, so that he might better be able to deal with the white man by knowing his tricks and the forked tongue with which he proposed them."[6] Most of the action and many of the characters' names in this tale derive from *The Brass Command*.

"Second Chance to Santa Fe" dramatizes the second chance of a nineteen-year-old, discredited civilian scout named Bass Cooper along the Santa Fe Trail. Earlier, a wagon train he was guiding was massacred by Pawnee Fork Comanche war chief Big Head and his followers. Even so, Bass is hired, though reluctantly, to replace an injured scout. The youth works extra hard to regain favor: he not only captures a stray Comanche but tortures him to learn where Big Head plans a fresh ambush. Successful in slaughtering the enemy and thus saving the wagons, Bass for good measure challenges the departing chief and snapshoots him to death at four hundred yards. This slight story is unlike Allen, since it minimizes the historical background. I find it hard to believe in the miraculous shot; even harder to credit is the fact that distant white witnesses heard "the soaplike swat of the huge [Sharps 400-grain] bullet going home." The best line in the story is Bass's Comanche challenge to Big Head: " 'Th-gyh-heu'bH!' " (52).

"River of Decision" retells the ending of *The Crossing*. In the novel Judah Beaumont "Jud" Reeves, III, left Sibley's shattered army, forgot his supposed love Felicia Horton, and crossed the Rio Grande to an Apache future with Apache half-breed Star. In the short story James Beaumont "Jim" Travis, III, quits the army after Sibley and Glorietta, forgets his supposed love Felicia Leeton, and crosses the same river to share his life with a bandit's daughter, Apache Nah-lin. The story elucidates two morals: " '[N]o war is ever won' " (63) and Don't look back.

"Legend of Trooper Hennepin" appears after "River of Decision," which is based on the ending of *The Crossing*. Hennepin's story is based on action early in *The Crossing*. Again, principal names are changed. In *The Crossing* Cavanaugh asks Jud to help him rescue his part-Apache daughter Star; in "Legend of Trooper Hennepin" Peckinpaugh asks Hennepin to help him rescue his half-Apache daughter Pilar. In the course of both rescue sequences major parallels abound, embarrassingly—until the end. The Allen afficionado knows exactly what to expect. Hennepin, like Jud before him, will cross that river, that color line, and that border to go native. Right? Wrong! Hennepin rescues Pilar all right, but will then marry her on the Fort Mimbres base and require her to go white-Christian.

Most oddly, then, Jud Reeves of *The Crossing* splits into Jim

Travis of "River of Decision," who goes native in Apacheria, and into Hennepin of "Legend of Trooper Hennepin," who persuades a native to go Christian.

"Lapwai Winter" is one of Allen's best short stories. It too is abstracted from a previous novel, *From Where the Sun Now Stands*. In the beautiful little tale Heyets, the Nez Percé narrator of the novel, is taken through his early teen-age troubles with the whites, is ordered to follow a carefree summer by reporting to the Christian missionary school at Lapwai in Idaho territory, which he does—for a while. Again, parallels between earlier novel and later tale are blatant. Read by itself, "Lapwai Winter" is magnificent. But it may be disappointing for the reader to learn that it is only a retelling of chapters 3-7 of *From Where the Sun Now Stands*.

Outlaws and Legends. The first two stories in *Outlaws and Legends* also derive from earlier long fiction by Allen. "Vengeance of Jesse James" tells us again that Jesse James when a vicious brat of eight shot an old dog to cover his tracks and those of his aghast cohorts Frank James and Cole Younger during the recapture of a freed slave. "Rough Riders of Arizona" retells the story of a young Arizona cowboy's efforts to join Teddy Roosevelt's volunteers at Fort Whipple, outside Prescott; in *San Juan Hill* the cowboy was Fate Beylen, whereas in "Rough Riders of Arizona" he is Pete Easter. In the short story a recruit's first days are described nicely, and some details, as well as several names, are changed; but the work seems weak and pointless, especially since this tale of a few youthful Rough Riders ends before they get to Cuba to ride rough.

"Ghost Wolf of Thunder Mountain," however, is another matter. This is one of Allen's most disturbing works, and a superb one. It bears serious if tangential comparison with Henry James's thriller "The Turn of the Screw," strange though that statement may sound. Each has a story within a story. Each narration is revealed during the Christmas season. Each has a strange little boy. Each makes oblique allusions to infernal powers. At this juncture the comparison breaks off: Allen's story concludes without ambiguity or the possibility of any rational explanation through assignment of hallucination to the main adult participant.

"Ghost Wolf of Thunder Mountain" is a ghost story, pure, simple, and haunting. In it the first narrator, who is a scientist and an expert on Western timber wolves, explains that he got the story he is about to reveal from a participant in its action. During Christmas time

at Don Gaspar de Portogo's Agua Piedra ranch in the New Mexican
Sangres region, the lupologist, a guest there, hears a fearful, sobbing
wolf-call rolling down El Trueno, Thunder Mountain. An old man,
also a guest, hears it too, breaks through the crust of his decades-old
memories, and tells the sympathetic scientist his tale at last. He was
once young, rich, happily married, and the father of one child only—
a son. The boy heard a wolf call, was lured by it into following, and
then had to be tracked by his father and his men. The boy's tiny footprints mingled with those of a gigantic panther, which was blessedly
found dead of a powerful throat swipe—from the wolf? The boy's
tracks and those of a wolf then trailed off, parallel to each other. The
father and his exhausted men tracked on and on, until the boy's
footprints led them back to the father's ranch. The lad was safe!
Soon, however, he began behaving so strangely that church and
medical consultants had to be summoned—to no avail. Was the wolf
exerting a satanic influence? At last the boy answered the call of
the wolf yet again; but this time, when the two were followed, their
tracks simply disappeared. The *anciano* who has been relating his son's
story to the scientist closes, complaining of extreme fatigue, by saying
that he will now join his long-dead son. Fireplace embers pop and
distract the scientist; turning back, he sees that the *anciano* is dead,
and smiling. The scientist steps outside, observes three sets of tracks
leading from the hacienda—those of old man, young lad, and huge
wolf—heading up toward El Trueno. He turns away, then looks again,
more closely; but by now the snow has effaced all evidence.[7]

Even better, perhaps, is the ghostly story called "A Bullet for
Billy the Kid." Read on one level, it is a factual narration of the life,
murderous deeds (I count nineteen killings), and death of infamous
Billy the Kid. But it has an overlay of supernaturalism: a curious
death figure, also partly a fate figure, named Asaph accompanies
Billy Bonney from birth through childhood with his ill-starred mother
into homicidal maturity to his rendezvous with Pat Garrett. Blandly
diabolical Asaph is impervious to bullets, and his gaunt, pale horse
leaves no tracks. Asaph can will the action of others by his mere
gaze, sometimes works his effects by issuing opposite advice, counsels
Garrett and his aides, nods as fate deals out events in accordance
with his stacking of the deck, and leads laughing Billy to an eternity
of hell fire.

Allen boldly corrects "untrue" aspects of the legend of Billy the
Kid. Thus, we read that Billy "never shot from the front or straight-

away, the legend notwithstanding" (57); a certain act "put the sure lie to the legend claiming Pat and Billy to be friends" (80); "[t]he legend goes that Billy grew hungry after deciding to bed down" at Pete Maxwell's fatal ranch, but the legend "did not match with Asaph's" (81); and "Asaph knew but never told" why Billy got up because Asaph "saw no need to say that Garrett lied," since a "lawman never tells all that he knows, or, if he does, he soon finds himself the victim of his own honesty" (82). In this ingenious manner Allen defies students of Western history: how can anyone argue with an immortal devil figure who stood constantly at fated Billy's very side?

Sources and analogues of "A Bullet for Billy" include William Shakespeare's *Hamlet*, Nathaniel Hawthorne's "Young Goodman Brown," Herman Melville's *Moby Dick*, Thornton Wilder's *The Bridge of San Luis Rey*, E. E. Cummings's "Buffalo Bill's Defunct," and Ira Levin's *Rosemary's Baby*. The most eerie stylistic technique in Allen's prose story is its use of innumerable sequences of blank verse. Of perhaps six or eight especially effective passages which might be noted, the following may be the best, as set in verse form:

> "Come, bony one," said Asaph softly to
> The horse. "We must not fall too far
> Behind, who would be there when needed most.
> The track turns north again before Roswell,
> And moonrise, two weeks hence. Fort Sumner is
> The way, I think. What was that name again?
> Tayban Arroyo? Why waste time with Garrett
> And his friends? We'll simply go and wait." (77)[8]

"Bandits of Tehuantltux," on the other hand, is a piece of harmless humor, in which a stupid cantina proprietor is flattered into becoming a bandit-gang leader. His attempt to steal horses—really burros—backfires; his followers are discommoded; and his would-be victim turns successful wine thief. Probably Allen's least effective story, even this one is enriched by wondrous dialogue, which is comic through including grotesque lacklogic.

"The Tallest Indian in Toltepec" is totally different, in spite of a title similar to "Bandits of Tehuantltux." The male Indian praised as tall is really only five feet: his stature elevates itself through his bravery. A sadistic "loyalist" Mexican colonel named Fulgencio Ortega is under orders at a Rio Grande crossing near Toltepec to shoot every available five-foot Mexican Indian, since El Indio (Benito Juarez), also five feet, is said to be trying to slip back into Mexico with gold from Abraham Lincoln to help Juarez's revolutionary cause. Plucky little Juliano is the right—rather, the wrong—size and hence is shot before the terrified gaze of his ten-year-old son Chamaco, who then escapes into the Rio Grande and is saved by Charlie Shonto (narrator of "The Hunting of Tom Horn"). The two get to El Paso, where they learn that El Indio is crossing secretly by stagecoach, hoping to catch the train from Toltepec down to Mexico City. With invaluable Chamaco becoming a pretty "tall" Indian himself, Shonto aids the Christlike revolutionary (also pretty "tall") in his gory dash south. In a rare published comment on his own fiction Allen calls this story a mythic, legendary, "quasi-factual . . . recreating [of] the . . . liaison between . . . Juarez and . . . Lincoln."[9]

Nine Lives West (1978).   *Nine Lives West* is a collection of nine stories, six of which were previously published in *The Oldest Maiden Lady in New Mexico and Other Stories*. Those six are "A Mighty Big Bandit," "The Redeeming of Fate Rachel," "King Fisher's Road," "The Trap," "The Hunting of Tom Horn," and "Sundown Smith." New between book covers are the following three: "The Streets of Laredo," "The Skinning of Black Coyote," and "For Want of a Horse."

"The Streets of Laredo" is another ghostly tale, akin to "The Trap." "The Streets of Laredo" stars wanted gunman McComas, already dead at story's start, although neither he nor the reader knows it. The gunman canters into town, observes a burial ceremony, sees a female mourner, goes to a bar and meets a gentle girl there, talks intimately with her about a possible future together, but then is called outside by the sheriff and duels fatally with him. He staggers to the waiting girl, who is oneirically holding his faithful mount Coaldust (a pun?) and who urges him to meet her at the cemetery. But it is she whom he saw there before. The climax is not confusing, only challenging and upsetting. "The Streets of Laredo" is remarkably crafted, has a Bierce touch or two, and may be a rehearsal for elements in the conclusion of *I, Tom Horn*. The moral of the story is that the much-touted American second chance is sometimes granted only beyond the cemetery.

"The Skinning of Black Coyote," new in book form, is a reworking of an episode from *Santa Fe Passage* (chapters 8 and 9). In the novel villain Tuss McLawry plots with chief Satank to kill hero Kirby Randolph and smuggle rifles. In "The Skinning of Black Coyote" for Kirby read Tracy Higgins, for Tuss read Tate, and for Kiowa Satank read Arapaho Black Coyote.

"For Want of a Horse" centers on the Jesse James gang's plan to rob a Missouri and Western train at Hatpin, Kansas. When the scheme starts to turn sour, because of some feisty civilians in town, Jesse orders the station telegraphist to wire a poised railroad detective and his ready men to bring some horses. After some bewildering action, Jesse and his stalwarts manage the robbery and escape on the the steeds thus freighted in. Curiously, Allen here romanticizes the James bunch, and this in spite of the fact that Cole Younger is not present but Charlie Pitts is. Frank James even quotes from "Bill" Shakespeare.

Children's Books

Allen might have made a lucrative career out of writing books for juvenile readers. He certainly knows a thousand yarns of the Old West. He also knows child psychology. In addition he can write uniquely well about animals. Further, he has a flair for the mysterious, the ghostly, and the wildly comic. If all of that is not a complex recipe for children's books, what is? But having published five excellent volumes for children, beginning in 1951—at the outset of his literary career—he stopped after 1965.

Wolf-Eye (1951). *Wolf-Eye* is a rousing book, and subtle as well. Believe it or not, but just as the heroes of *No Survivors* and *Red Blizzard*, the only books by Allen to precede *Wolf-Eye* into print, are psychically divided into white and red, civilized and pagan, so is the hero of *Wolf-Eye*. This splendid animal is nominally a German shepherd, in the Great Mogollon Mesa area of Arizona, but has atavistic wolf blood in him. Accordingly, he is not only loyal to his owner, rancher Jim Lewis, but also willing to answer the immemorial voice of the wilderness. When Jim tries to train Wolf-Eye as a cowherder, the dog overzealously tears an obstreperous steer's throat out. Further, when the wind blows free and brings Wolf-Eye the scent of Vega, a lovely she-wolf, he answers the call of the wild, goes native, and sires a fine litter. Yet Wolf-Eye still loves Jim and even steals one of his gloves as a memento. Summer drought turns the wolf family ravenous, and Wolf-Eye, its leader, must drag down the ranchers' cattle for food. The region is soon up in arms, and with hunting dogs to boot. In a complex conclusion the animal hero is faced with a choice: should he follow his savage yearnings or save the life of unforgotten, injured Jim? Allen uses a lupine point of view in a Jamesian manner here; describes animal appearances, actions, and even thoughts with great skill; treats animal matings cleanly and tenderly; and includes such harmless Western expletives ("Good grief!," "Holy Cow!," "Holy smoke!," and "Man alive!") that not even the foxiest PTA library-committee persons could find fault.

The Texas Rangers (1957).   *The Texas Rangers* is Allen's most historically oriented book for children. It is well organized in three parts: the Texas Rangers against the Comanches, 1835-40; the Rangers against Mexican banditti, 1842-74; and the Rangers against American outlaws, 1874-78. The scenes vary but only from Texas to Oklahoma and Mexico. Action is strictly unified: the Rangers always respond, never retreat, never surrender (well, almost never), and expect little or no reward; they are always tougher than their enemies, and even tougher than more formal American military units. Allen is informative, often funny, never supercilious. Nor does he gloss over shameful aspects in America's past. The famous Texas Rangers are—or were for young readers in the 1950s—exemplary role models. Sadly, the book might be regarded by some as too violent for young readers today.

Allen includes a bibliography and made special use of Walter Prescott Webb's *The Texas Rangers*, Stanley Vestal's *Bigfoot Wallace*, and J. Frank Dobie's *The Flavor of Texas*. The author cannot resist putting his tongue in his cheek and informing his young readers, in much the way he does adults on occasion, that he simply had to supply some details and descriptions on his own hook because many official records have been destroyed by fire. An interesting aside: Allen laments the fact that "Tom Horn, another bad man, has become an Outlaw Saint on the Great Plains."[10]

Orphan of the North (1958).   The hero of *Orphan of the North* is a moose named Awklet, orphaned during a wolf attack led by vicious, one-eyed Loki. Awklet is adopted by a philosophical caribou mother named Neetcha and grows up to become the caribou herd's leader. Once mature, Awklet is massive, towering, brave, and as resourceful as any Apache raider.

Orphan of the North is an artistic narrative. It is unified by locale and seasonal cycles, balanced shifts in point of view (from caribou to wolf and back and forth), rhythmic military movements from defense to offense, and possibly an underlying allegory. It is intriguing to interpret Awklet and his friends as symbolic of doomed Indians, scared, puzzled, drifting into occasional disunity, and the wolves as emblematic of ever-advancing white "civilization," armed in a superior manner, and jealous of the caribous' all-nurturing natural sanctuary, which is given a metaphorical name—Hemlock Wood.

The most resounding stylistic success of this acclaimed book for youngsters[11] must surely be Allen's getting into the dying consciousness of Loki the villain, in a sequence reminiscent of the celebrated conclusion of Lytton Strachey's *Queen Victoria*. Young readers ought, however, to remember longer Allen's gently inculcated morals here: it is often necessary to fight for freedom; nature never coddles the weak but instead helps those who help themselves; leaders must study the trail ahead; even giants can be brought low; and you cannot win by running away too far.

Valley of the Bear (1964). *Valley of the Bear* (a particular favorite of Allen's—A to G, 7/11/81) has a fine plot line, which concerns an Oglala Sioux youth named Tonkalla (Mouse) and his peppery, half-cracked old grandmother Ousta (Limper). Banished from their tribe for befriending a supposedly malevolent bear in the mountains, Tonkalla and the crone make their way to a beautiful valley in those same mountains. They set up residence in a log cabin abandoned by white hunters. But soon their little paradise is threatened: evil Patch Eye enters, hired by the Sioux to kill the bear. The rest of the story tells how Tonkalla defends the bear with his spunky grandma's aid.

The story is neatly structured. The first fifteen chapters tell of Tonkalla's banishment to the valley. In the next three chapters Patch Eye is sighted, is cannily prepared for by old Ousta, and enters. The last sixteen chapters detail his horrifying plans and fatal discomfiture. Throughout, the novel is spiced with pungent humor. When Tonkalla, who is "no heavier than a wet saddle,"[12] becomes frightened at one point, his "blood turned to weed juice" (17). Ousta grins a lot, thus "showing her three remaining teeth to excellent advantage" (45). She lets her grandson's best friend smoke her pipe and then explains that her tobacco mixture includes " 'yucca soapweed and a pinch of dried buffalo chips' " (40). Tonkalla proudly acquires the ability to swear, "and he owed it all to gentle little Ousta. . . . Such a grandmother was a true gift"(83). The old woman upbraids Patch Eye

thus: " 'You stink like a wet dog in a warm tipi' " (97). After all,
Ousta, unlike "[t]he real crazy" Patch Eye, is "the rambling happy
kind of crazy" (120) that kids usually tolerate and often like.

Associating with Ousta, Tonkalla learns many valuable lessons:
worry about life not death; don't coddle the weak too much; make
your own decisions; take the rougher trail rather than the easier one;
and pray a lot to Watan Tanka (Sioux for God). Interestingly, Allen
took the name Ousta from that of the villainous squaw in *Warbonnet*;
named the bear's mountain Sotoju (Smoke) after Murrah Starr's wolf
Sotaju in *The North Star*; and would tell us more in "Peace of the
Pony Soldiers" (included in *The Last Warpath*) about Tonkalla,
who, when grown into adulthood, aids Crazy Horse, He Dog, and
Two Moons.

In the Land of the Mandans (1965).   Allen's last book for
children is *In the Land of the Mandans*, which uniquely has a respected white character successfully debate with an Indian boy on the
advantage of white justice over Indian justice—with manifest authorial
approval. Little Raven, the boy hero of the story, is descended from
York, Shahaka, and Sacajawea from Lewis and Clark days (and from
The Gates of the Mountains). He undertakes to get evidence that
Assiniboin-descended medicine man Knife Eye is smuggling Canadian
whiskey into the starving Mandan village and illegally hoarding food
bought with the sordid proceeds. Little Raven succeeds but is in
danger of being killed by Knife Eye, until he is rescued by Sergeant
"Red Coat" Mackenzie of the Royal Canadian Mounties. Now the
debate. Little Raven favors turning the red-handed villain over to the
Mandans. But, says Mackenzie, they " 'would kill him without a fair
trial. They would strip him naked and drive him out into the snow
to freeze to death.' " To the rejoinder that the criminal deserves no
less, the policeman agrees but still voices his preference for a fair trial
first, before any punishment. The boy calls white law " 'strange' " and
adds that " '[t]he Indian way is better; it is much quicker.' " Mackenzie
ends the debate thus: " 'Quicker and better are not the same, lad . . .
Slow and sure is the way the white man's justice works.' "[13] This
seems odd in light of much of Allen's other fiction.

In the Land of the Mandans is suspenseful and busy, just the
sort of book that most kids love to read. Delightfully, on three arith-
metically spaced occasions, Little Raven escapes Knife Eye by axing
fiercely at the villain's toes (chapters 8, 17, 27). The feeling of
bitter-cold winter pervades every chapter. Memorable is Allen's use

of the Romulus and Remus story, when the little hero hides in a wolf den with a wolf family. We read that "the Indian boy was hungry, and when his stomach began to draw in small from emptiness, he lay down with his new brothers and sisters, the wolf whelps, and took his supper as they did. The mother wolf was pleased at this. She turned her head and bumped Little Raven with her nose and licked him with her tongue just as she did her own children" (41).

Allen's books for children are rough and honest and fun, like a good parent. They are best when they show that life can be difficult, but that resourceful kids, and animals too, can make it if they persevere.

Now and Future Outlaws

Henry Allen seemingly could not exhaust his versatility by writing of the Old West in fiction long and short; so he also wrote a novel about escaped convicts in a contemporary setting and for good measure a science-fiction thriller set in the twenty-first century.

See How They Run (1970). *See How They Run* is exciting but not significant to an understanding of Allen. It shows his versatility but does not illustrate his essential value, which is that of a commentator on the Old Western scene. In a forced sense, *See How They Run* may be regarded as a formulaic western novel: it features an embattled hero against a kind of frontier society, a self-sacrificial sidekick, a pathetic "soiled-dove" heroine, a corrupt young lawman trying to dislodge a decent old one, and a manhunt set in an oppressive natural setting and imaged as a deadly game.

The story is about the loyalty of Roan Hawks, a Texan in his mid-thirties, who is a Korean War veteran and now an escaped convict, and fellow-escapee Pettus Yantley, Roan's huge black friend from their cotton-picking days on the Hawkses' Sweetgum County family farm. The story centers on their effort to evade the police, led by a redneck deputy named Linkwell "Link" Wade, whose more humane boss cannot restrain him. The convicts, together with a third fugitive, happen upon a Tobacco Road-type swamp shack in which Carrie Lassiter, a seventeen-year-old single girl, has just given birth to a Mongoloid baby boy—all by herself. Rather crazily, Allen converts this early episode into a grotesque Christ story: three wise cons seeking a star to guide them, oppressed new mother with real father absent, and all on December 24; Carrie even prays to Jesus, recalls

Joseph and his mule, and rides her own mule for supplies to help injured Roan and his friends.

In a lengthy aside we learn that Link shot a hostage whom the three convicts had grabbed during their robbery of a bank just after they broke out. Link did this on purpose because the victim was the wild college-boy cause of Carrie's pregnancy, and Link has the slavering hots himself for the comely girl. When the third convict turns into a yellow traitor, Pettus stabs him to death but is caught in the process. Carrie gets Roan, whom she hopelessly loves, to the temporary sanctuary of a nightmarish swamp community controlled by a strange black family: tough Granny Clune, her widower son Noah, and his three sons, Shem, Ham, and Japheth. Jap, a fire-crippled Vietnamese War medical-corps veteran who has long loved white Carrie hopelessly, cures Roan and is practically labeled tragic loser from the first.

It is impossible to summarize the subsequent plot complications here. We have selfless friendship, unspeakable vileness, much commentary on racism, and Hollywood-serial episodic melodrama. The book is constructed in circular form: the first eleven chapters make a wide arc, followed by an epicycle of three vital chapters; then the last ten chapters complete the circle, and the action ends where it all started. The whole is unified partly by the device of grotesque football imagery emanating from the depraved consciousness of Link. The book has one of Allen's finest religious lines. When Roan asks Pettus whether he has been praying and receives the answer " 'Been trying,' " he goes on: " 'Asking or thanking?' "[14]

Genesis Five (1968). *Genesis Five*, Allen's chilling horror story of Soviet genetic experimentation in twenty-first-century Siberia, can be read as a sci-fi western, if you please. The hero is Yuri U. Suntar, a crypto-Christian Mongolian throwback descended from Tamerlane, and now a student of politics in Moscow. He is tardily considered dangerous because he believes in God and has a sense of humor. He must stop a mad Chinese scientist named Dr. Ho Wu Chen from combining bees (for their hardworking sociability), wolves (for their murderous propensities), and human beings (for their big brains) by mutation through genetic engineering into hiving, lethal, intelligent larvanoids. They are to be let loose from Dr. Ho's arctic laboratory beneath the polar ice cap to depopulate the world. Thereafter the super-race (i.e., Sino-Russo Reds) can inherit a less crowded planet.

Yuri is sent to the arctic region by unsuspecting authorities to calm down the giant Yang Suntar, his twin brother, who is normally capable of controlling the needed wolf packs thereabouts but is now upset.[15] Once up there, Yuri assembles a subversive squad to help him, James Bond-like, to shut down the lab. His colorful cohorts include a stunning female Afro-Oriental spaceship pilot named Chana Meru Maringa, her tough Massai father (Simba), a bright and delightful Finn (Kano Komuli), a defecting Russian general (Ket), and—truth to tell—Moshe Dyan's tough grandnephew (Lev Dyan Eshman).

Since science fiction is hardly Allen's forte, we need not spend much more time on *Genesis Five*. However, it is an authentic thriller, has a hero possessed of American Indian attributes, is competently managed from beginning to end, is absorbing, and is narrated with clinical detachment. Every scene is meticulously sketched. Allen does nothing less than provide a scenario that could be translated to the wide screen with minimal rewriting and maximum explosive success. Our indomitable crew zap enemy headquarters and then lift off with true Double O Seven panache. But trouble develops. Then Allen draws upon his experience as author of *No Survivors, I, Tom Horn*, and other westerns which start and/or end with the recovery of preserved documents.

In the final analysis, Yuri Suntar, hero of *Genesis Five*, is not unlike a daring young Sitting Bull summoning intertribal cohorts, overseeing the massacre of Custer and the Seventh Cavalry, and then riding off toward Canada. What is left behind to tell Yuri's whole truth and not too much but it? The snow-covered journal of Cetan Mani? No. The true confessions of Tom Horn? No. Pictographs perhaps? No. Only a twenty-first-century voiceprint. But Allen does not jest here. In *Genesis Five* he suggests that our civilization can easily go the way of the buffalo and the Mandan if we let ourselves be overcome by an alien so-called civilization.

Criticism

Allen would be the last man to say that he is a literary critic. He rarely preaches what he often practices. That is, he rarely offers published comments on his craft or that of colleagues, admired, imitative, or hostile. All the same, a little collection of dicta by him might be assembled.

In 1968 Allen edited a Bantam Books collection of short stories written by members of the Western Writers of America. It is called

14 Spurs; and Allen also provided an Introduction, in which he opts for life over art, praises "the traditional western story" when it "presents a precut slice of homespun life which is a gallant trial of good against evil in a perilous time and place where bravery and clean intent will not be matched by cowardice or dishonor" (viii), declares his abiding love for "[t]he folklore story . . . with overtones of puckishness or pathos" (ix), and laments the passing of the Old West. All of which is little but an implicit definition of his own practice.

In his "Breaking Ground for a Novel" Allen offers a controversial recipe, with tongue partly in cheek, for writing a good western novel. One should first read much Western history, taking notes while doing so; collect memorabilia about Western people, processes, weapons, horses, and the like; and then pick a topic—that is the easy part—pray that you have a modicum of talent and will be lucky, and start writing.

"Guarding the Packline to the Past" is Allen's ebullient appeal to fellow Western Writers of America to stay on the right side of the wavering line between legitimate violence and unacceptable pornography. Too many current adult westerns are devoid of "humor or satire or high camp," Allen avers. Too many have "no art, no quality, no socially redeeming significance." Instead, they display "plain unfunny fornication from page one to page last."[16] The resulting "Shortarm Syndrome" "disfigure[s] the humanity of our frontier times," "infect[s] the integrity of our folklore," and is fast rendering "the Western an endangered species" (7).

Many critics agree. They, as well as millions of readers, come back again and again to Allen's—criticism? No!—his practice. When Allen practices his craft best, he illustrates what most contemporary critics are preaching for when they—and he—preach against much in the post-Allen western.

And in "Will Henry and the Indians" Allen thumbs his nose at unsympathetic academicians and reviewers; sides instead with romantic humanists; defines his Indian works as "historical novels"[17] which avoid stereotyping Indians as either always perfect or always dastardly; but then proudly asserts that he "pens an eulogy with every book he writes of them" (13), and even expresses a wish that he had "been born a horseback Indian of the high plains, riding wild and free and forever away from the haunts of the white man" (10-11); and closes

with a quiet boast that his "eulogy" will outlast the pronouncements
of "down-beat truth-twisters" (13), that is, hypocritical ideologists.
You tell 'em, *Wasicun.*

Chapter Eight
Style and Message

Henry W. Allen is a unique stylist. Every Western writer is distinctive, and perhaps a typical work by any good one could be identified by an expert or an afficionado. But great numbers of such writers fall into schools or subgenres, and their styles are somewhat interchangeable. Allen, however, is sole and incomparable, as William Dean Howells said of Mark Twain. Further, in my opinion, the literary quality of a typical Will Henry work—for example, *The Bear Paw Horses*—is not materially different from that of a representative Clay Fisher effort, say, *The Big Pasture.*

Allen's manner takes getting used to. The first stylistic features striking new readers are his often edgy tone, sometimes bordering on an affected surliness, his ribby humor, his discontent with standard sources and preference for oral tradition, even legend, and an apparent loosening of tight structure by a seeming inclination toward the casual and the rambling. But be not deceived. Allen is a writers' writer, and his possibles sack is bulging with rhetorical weapons and gadgets.

Style

Almost without exception, titles of Allen's works are excellent. For example, *Red Blizzard* suggests assault by Indians in winter. *Who Rides with Wyatt* not only stresses the proximity of death wherever Wyatt Earp goes but also hints that throughout the action Johnny Ringo, the novel's enigma, should be watched. The title of *Journey to Shiloh* prefigures its rites-of-passage action: greenhorns leaving home will be initiated by lurid combat into maturity—and worse. *The Feleen Brand* may hint at an older brand than ever seared a steer, that of Cain. Other examples might be cited. Sometimes titles suggest places, not action; thus, *The Big Pasture, The Crossing, The Gates of the Mountains, Valley of the Bear.* Occasionally place and action are jammed together, as with *Santa Fe Passage, The Seven Men at Mimbres Springs, The Day Fort Larking Fell.* Curiously, "The Outcasts of Poker Flat," one of the best stories of Bret Harte, an Allen favorite, would seem to have inspired, however subterraneously, two Allen titles whose plots are contiguous: *Reckoning at Yankee Flat* and *Outcasts of Canyon Creek.* Only a few of the titles Allen gave to his works seem ineffective; they include *The Pitchfork Patrol, The Last Warpath, Alias Butch Cassidy,* and possibly *The Squaw Killers* (the squaws were not killers but victims). Among the finest titles Allen devised are *No Survivors, Orphan of the North, In the Land of the Mandans, Genesis Five, Apache Ransom,* and especially *The Crossing* and *One More River to Cross.* They are provocative, overture-like, often poetic and rhythmic.

The subject of Allen's use of sources is enormous, complex, and ultimately baffling. It would take a competent Western historian who was willing to sort "fact" from fiction, distinguish between oral tradition and tribal legend, in order for any definitive word on the score to appear. Even then, one radically disturbing problem would remain. Allen himself is contradictory, is of two minds, for a few examples, with respect to Custer, Tom Horn, Montana vigilantes, and even the Apache psyche.

The novelist writes of the "[p]otholes in the stage road of all journeys between tribal lore and the white man's hard history" (*Chiricahua,* 239). The image is illuminating. It positions the author between two cultures, literally between two schools, and perhaps implies that he is awkwardly transporting discrete cargoes and maybe shaken passengers—to wit, paying readers.

Apart from certain respected sources, Allen distrusts the white record. To begin with, history cannot explain everything even now. About one episode in *The Fourth Horseman* we read that "[t]he questions are as unanswered today as they were in their own time. The known fact ... has had only one explanation—one put forward years later by a surviving . . . partisan" (127). Further, some accounts vary, as with dates of certain events in Isom Dart's life (*One More River to Cross,* 76). Many a skirmish important to Allen and his stories fails to "appear in the published military record" (*Chiricahua,* 242), some through being too humiliating to the army (*The Squaw Killers,* 27). Certain important places even fail to turn up on official maps; thus Allen notes that "Fort Larking does not appear on the maps of western Kansas today," adding cheekily that "[t]here is a good reason for that" (*The Day Fort Larking Fell,* v).

Over and over Allen uses white history but in case of doubt prefers Indian tradition or legend for clarification. For one comprehensive example, in his epilogue to *Apache Ransom* (148) Allen explains that "[w]hite historians tend to consider the four hostile bands, Nednhi, Bedonkohe, Warm Springs, and True Chiricahua as, in fact, all Chiricahuan peoples. Some Indians differ. James Kaywaykla, Warm Springs Apache . . . , writes: 'I say *peoples*, although the White Eyes designated the members of all four different Apache bands as Chiricahua. This was an error . . . Though closely associated, we were distinct groups." Or—more briefly—"[s]peaking . . . in the summer of 1915 . . . Two Moons, then over seventy years old and straight as a sapling pine, had this to say of the [1866] Battle of the Bozeman Crossing of the Yellowstone" (*The Tall Men*, 184), etc. A white man's reminiscence might count, particularly if the fellow were old and self-incriminatory. Thus Frank James, years later, "balanced history's books" by confessing the size of a sum swiped decades before (*The Raiders*, 139). Allen does not hesitate to call even a legend wrong. For example, did Fate Rachel wave farewell to the little family he saved? Allen notes that "[i]t was the way they told it in any case. But it was not the true way" ("The Redeeming of Fate Rachel," in *The Oldest Maiden Lady in New Mexico*, 104).

How should a person write in the absence of definitive documentation? Allen has a formula: "After all, where memory fails, fabrication will do as well. Ofttimes better" (*Black Apache*, 118). He also complexly suggests at least once that people in the present can choose to act in such a way as to make a legend inherited from the past come true (*Tayopa!*, 176-77).

The narrative voice in many of Allen's novels and stories is that of an old codger, one who has been through the dust, mud, blood, and fun of varied Western experience. He is often weary but seldom cynical. He is old-fashioned, crotchety, full of quiet wisdom, and gets a kick out of exaggerating in a tall-tale fashion—not to deceive but to intrigue the auditor.

I cannot guess whether Allen likes young people and, therefore, writes sometimes as though perched on an adolescent's shoulder, or sees Western adventure as the province of youth and, therefore, follows mostly the young into action. In either event, the heroes of *The Blue Mustang, The Crossing, From Where the Sun Now Stands, Journey to Shiloh, San Juan Hill, The Feleen Brand, The Gates of the Mountains, Alias Butch Cassidy,* and *Summer of the Gun* are young. Often their wrenchingly fast maturing provides the poignant drama.[1]

Allen handles the technical aspects of point of view with versatility. He sometimes shifts point of view as only an omniscient narrator or a movie director with several camera crews might do. For a simple example, in chapter 15 of *The North Star* we first see villain McClennon and his vicious men and second move into heroine Erin's gentle memories of Murrah Starr. More elaborate are the first three chapters of *Yellow Hair*: first, we meet the hero Kelso; second, his Indian enemy Mad Wolf; and third, their common white challenge, Custer. Only an omniscient narrator could spirit us about so fast. Sometimes, as in *Mackenna's Gold*, chapter 29, and *One More River to Cross*, chapters 52 and 66, Allen shifts point of view with unaccustomed awkwardness. But pretty regularly he handles the first-person narrative point of view with skill and gusto. This is to be expected, since some of his best yarns purport to be eyewitness accounts or to come from preserved journals. For many examples, *No Survivors*, *The Blue Mustang*, *Reckoning at Yankee Flat*, *From Where the Sun Now Stands*, "Lapwai Winter," "King Fisher's Road," "The Hunting of Tom Horn," "A Mighty Big Bandit," *The Gates of the Mountains*, "Ghost Wolf of Thunder Mountain," *Genesis Five*, *Apache Ransom* and its sequel *Black Apache*, and *I, Tom Horn*. More often than not, the narrator is a participant but not very heroic, and, therefore, demeans himself engagingly. Exceptions occur in *No Survivors*, *Genesis Five*, and *I, Tom Horn*, whose autobiographical heroes are heroic, know it, and say so.

Perhaps the most remarkable manipulation of point of view in all of Allen appears in the opening segment of *Red Blizzard*, chapter 2, when this daring novelist describes Indians and soldiers separately approaching To-Ke-Ya, the dog fox, who listens carefully, notes what he hears, but then returns to business, catching a mouse. This is novelistic largesse, gratuitous stylistic dazzle.

It is manifest throughout his writings that Allen loves the Far West, from its chill northern reaches to torrid Apacheria, and all topographical and climatic varieties in between. He offers us spectacular visions of his beloved West, some of which have already been noted. Here are two more, both simple, chosen from among dozens of available verbal color slides. "The fair weather held. Late that afternoon, in a lovely small meadow of springs and hock-high forage, fringed by small timber and huge, house-high boulders, they made a happy camp. . . . [T]he strange green daylight of the late afternoon and early evening held on . . ." (*Return of the Tall Man*, 170, 171). And this:

In the sunset, the approach to the crossing was spectacular. To the north the great bent bow of the Orange Cliffs were dyed a fiery crimson. Southward the eight-thousand-foot guardian rampart of Mount Holmes reared snow-capped in a sky of wild pink and blue cloud floating against the twilight green of the winter day's end. Across the river, the great wash of White Canyon's mouth spewed itself into the Colorado, building the footing of unseen sand and rock which here widened and slowed the larger stream. . . . On the western shore, where George [Butch] Cassidy and Matt Warner now rode, the entire cliff formation of the main canyon drew back like some gigantic sandstone stage drop, to disclose . . . awesome stillness and majesty. . . . (*Alias Butch Cassidy*, 93)

If sound effects are required, Allen is never lacking. Hush Feleen, restless one moonlit night on the *brasada*, cocks his keen ear and hears longhorns "in their grunting brushtalk," an owl "hooting forlornly," a vixen "nickering spitefully," and a fox "scolding yappily in return"; then "the distant coughings of *el tigre*," a Mexican jaguar, and "the minor-keyed complaining of *lobo cano*, the gray dog-wolf, baying to the stars his discontent with doing all the meat hunting" for his bitch and whelps (*The Feleen Brand*, 60).

Allen is a master characterizer. He sets his dramatis personae before us by direct, photographic description. Like Luke Short and most other Western novelists, he depicts by limning eyes. He also uses crisp dialogue. And he tells us much about his characters through their handling of weapons and responses to dumb animals.

Behold General Nelson Miles. "He was an absolute soldier's soldier; tall, broad-shouldered, strong, flat-bellied, erect, bold-faced. In the prime of middle life, he had about him that unmistakable 'look of eagles' which the Prussian militarists so proudly ascribe to those rarest of war's aristocrats, the born field commanders" (*Yellowstone Kelly*, 165). Murrah Starr is even tougher:

His skin was the color of cordovan boot leather. The bony structure beneath it was as savagely cut and shadowed as a Kotzebue ivory carving. His hair, shoulder-long and coarse as a bear's, reached back from his low forehead in a shaggy blue-black mane. His nose and mouth were out of an aboriginal skin painting; the former as big and cruelly bridged as a fishhawk's beak; the latter as warm and pleasant as a knife slash. Only in his strangely blue eyes was there any hopeful hint of a possible white heritage. And even that slight chance was hedged by the high-boned Mongol slant with which their peculiar blue brilliance was set into the copper-dark mounting of his alien face. (*The North Star*, 68)

Feared Juh of *Apache Ransom* is an eyeful, too. Padre Nunez, narrator, sketches him in such lines as these: "Juh uttered a grunt. Glancing at him, I saw the gargoyle's beak of his face break into what had to be a Nednhi grin" (7). Curiously late in *Black Apache*, Allen paints a picture of the West Pointer turned Apache, black Flicker: 6′ 2″ or 3″ tall, without fat but neither lean nor gaunt, with Apache *h'deh h'keh* boots, Mexican vaquero trousers, American cavalry coat with buttons and chevrons, cap of savage hair only (cut each summer with sheep shears), and lion-like face.

Women in Allen's fiction are young and beautiful, young but overworked, and old and overworked. His first fictional dream woman is his most glorious and sets a standard for all successive ones. She is Star of the North, heroine of *No Survivors*, and she is depicted with Persian lushness: her face "was oval in outline, as true and sure in its form as a master's sketch. The skin was waxy and petal-clear, the hue of a virgin copper vein broken asunder in subterranean darkness, glowing with its own dusky inner fires, carrying within its velvet self a living bloom of copper-gold. The eyes were long, lashed with charcoal blackness and set ever so slightly aslant by the high-curving line of the cheekbones. Their color a clear, depthless green, at once as cold as north sea ice and hot as the fire in an emerald's heart" (60). Her other features, all in harmony, are lovingly lingered on: nose, chin, mouth (with "snow-clean teeth," 93), ears, hair, fragrance, neck, shoulders, waist, breasts, hips, legs, calves, ankles, feet, hands, lips, fingers, and laugh. Francie Stanton, central female of *Mackenna's Gold,* is also sketched tantalizingly: white, young, scared, tortured, attractive, resolute at last. The most grotesque female in all of Allen must be Simialita (Monkey Woman, Little Monkey), the mother of depraved Santiago Kifer and Niño Bonito of *Black Apache.* When Nunez first sees her, "she was engaged in picking fat gray lice from her rancid hair and cracking them in her teeth." Nunez decides to be brief: "Not to squander charity, . . . what a vile and greasy woman" (177).

A "former journeyman scenarist" (A to G, 4/6/82), Allen learned his craft well, forgot filmic excess, and has offered in his best fiction a thousand passages of superb dialogue. Understatement is common and effective, as is to be expected in most well-written Western fiction. Another common type of funny talk features mangled pronunciation (" ' . . . any contract signed under durast ain't legal and blinding' "—*Alias Butch Cassidy*, 118) and malapropisms (" ' . . . them colored fellers is pretty superstitched' "—*One More River to Cross*, 136). But Allen elevates his dialogue above that of ordinary Western writers in three main ways: Jamesian rhythms, comic scatology, and hyperbolic good fun.

In one long, tense conversation Sergeant Schlonager and his corporal in *The Pitchfork Patrol* pick up on key words one from the other in a way reminiscent of talk in Henry James's major fiction. Here is a sample snippet: " 'The question is, *where?*' 'Where, *what?*' . . . 'No, . . . all I've got are my orders.' 'Your *orders!*' " (55).[2]

Dirty talk, often washed out a bit with cleansing laughter, runs through much of Allen, especially in *Red Blizzard, The Day Fort Larking Fell, Tayopa!, See How They Run, Chiricahua, The Bear Paw Horses, Apache Ransom, I, Tom Horn, Black Apache*, and *Summer of the Gun*. Subjects generating such talk include animals, bosoms, genitalia, elimination (solid, liquid, and gaseous), fear, fatigue, extremes of weather, food, and alcohol.

Without doubt, the funniest passage of dialogue in all of Allen occurs in *San Juan Hill*, when one soldier waxes critical of camp moonshine: " 'For mine . . . I would rather gargle with panther sign and goat gland oil than to take another swaller of that swill you cook up. That is the goddamnedest throat reamer I've ever come acrost in my sonofabitching life' " (97). In *Apache Ransom* the kidnap victim Little Buck—"dirty of mind like all healthy little boys," as Allen explains tolerantly—tells Father Nunez that he could not be the lad's father. The explanation is out of the ordinary: " 'Because priests don't have no peckers,' he told me soberly" (106).

Another dialogical tag is Allen's dazzling use of foreign words. They are mostly Indian but include a dash of Spanish and a pinch of French. The author employs great skill in unobtrusively defining them, thus educating the willing reader and adding to the sense of verisimilitude. A full list of such words and phrases would be long, but the following are a few busy ones: *anh, hijo, hotoma, mano à mano, métis, nohetto, puha, schichobe, Tejanos, ugashe, wonunicun*, and *woyuonihan*. And the ever-popular *Wagh!*

In at least two other clever ways, Allen characterizes. He judges many of his people by the manner in which they handle weapons and animals. Stark and his men break up a wild Indian attack late in *The Big Pasture* with four carbines, each with seven rounds, "caliber 52-56 Spencer, rimfire copper case"; when the redskin remnant pull back out of carbine range, "Chicksaw . . . stacked his Spencer and hauled out his old Sharps bullgun and drilled one of them clean at 450 yards . . . That buck had been so far away he looked like a tickbird sitting on a buffalo chip" (179). On a perilous rescue mission Cetan Mani must ride his noble horse Hussein to blind exhaustion, and we read: "Staggering brokenly, then finding his stride, he managed a racking whicker. His neck then, at the spot my face lay against it, was wet not from lather alone" (*No Survivors*, 125).

For all his scurrying between history and legend, his pauses to admire the scenery, his cinematic action and talk, and his guns and his beasts, Allen builds his best works with the precision of a master carpenter. He uses several devices to make his structures firm. One is to let the reader know the dates of major plot parts. Another is to pace a given action by moon-phase changes or a sequence of deaths. Yet another is to combine foreshadowing with statements to the effect that something the reader might anticipate will in fact not occur. Then again Allen employs the refrain technique. In many works he suspends forward movement, takes a breather, and summarizes what has been transpiring. This practice is especially tactful in fiction marked by plot intricacies or breakneck speed.

Perhaps the most obvious structuring technique in Allen is his blocking out his fictions into equal fractions, usually halves but not always. At many a halfway point pivotal action develops. Felicitous examples abound. At the end of chapter 13 of the twenty-seven-chapter *Yellow Hair* an amatory change occurs. In chapter 16 of *The Blue Mustang*, which has thirty-two chapters, the hero is abruptly left with no family support. Chapter 17 of *Return of the Tall Man*, which has thirty-three chapters, is entitled "Lost Sister" and describes the hero's first sight of the object of his quest, which object he immediately loses; the quest must continue. Exactly halfway through *The Feleen Brand* the flawed hero succumbs to his worst temptation— and is doomed. The twenty-first chapter of forty-two-chapter *Mackenna's Gold* describes the ambush of the black soldiers, after which there is no turning back. In the exact middle of "A Bullet for Billy the Kid" Pat Garrett first appears.

Several other novels fall into equal thirds (*The Raiders, Reckoning at Yankee Flat*), quarters (*The Feleen Brand*),[3] fifths (*Yellowstone Kelly, From Where the Sun Now Stands*), and even sixths (*Mackenna's Gold*). Still others, however, boast an informal, picturesque sprawl, either with (*Alias Butch Cassidy*) or without (*One More River to Cross*) parts numbered so as to claim otherwise. More interesting, however, than fractions in Allen's structures is the fact that distinct halves may symbolize the author's motivation in taking two pen names. Deep down, why did he? Did he wish to be both historically accurate and imaginative, inventive? I think so, even though he often manufactured Henrys and Fishers with interchangeable nuts and bolts. It is of interest, too, that Allen can be both prosaic and poetic. Late in *Red Blizzard* a Cheyenne and then a Sioux report the approach of white troops. The reports are identical substantively but distinct as to style: "The only difference . . . was the natural one [Allen comments] between a Cut Arm [Cheyenne] dullard and a Throat Slitter [Sioux] poet" (163). Perhaps Henry vs. Fisher? Better, perhaps Allen combines both Cheyenne exposition and Sioux lyricism, at his best.

Allen normally ends his narrations with old-fashioned closures. History often provides him the real fact, but he is wont to add a twist of mystery. Thus Schlonager (*The Pitchfork Patrol*) and the drifter (*Chiricahua*) turn enigmatic, as they wander away. Or Allen includes terminal footnotes that partly clarify but really tease the mind into still further speculation (*I, Tom Horn, Black Apache*). Best of all, he charmingly strings time out so as to connect his nineteenth-century events with twentieth-century rememberers of things past (*The Tall Men, Who Rides with Wyatt, The Seven Men at Mimbres Springs*). Almost never does a reader end an Allen fiction without pausing, scratching his head, and musing.

A distinctive feature of these novels is their imagery. Far and away the winner is poker tropes. Of the scores available, here is a typically straight one: "Pelón glanced around at his group. He had not yet played his hidden card, and was only being sure that it still lay buried in the deck. . . . The big white man [Mackenna], his raise checked, stood stock-still" (*Mackenna's Gold*, 84). *Outcasts of Canyon Creek* has a string of poker metaphors, including these: "The pasteboards were already face-down here." "But Ben's hole card did not . . . depend on a starve-out." "It was cards to the gamblers again." "Four vigilantes dead: one . . . blasted down out of a cold-deck surround . . ." And " 'Pick up the pot, Ruel. . . .' "[4]

Animal and hunting imagery is frequent and, given appropriate plot conditions, often exciting. The saddest human lion is Frank Rachel of *The Fourth Horseman*, caged by circumstance, anxious to be free again, even if it means leaping murderously on a would-be helper, coldly eyeing all.[5] Jesse James's saga, *The Raiders*, has apt imagery deriving from hunting, weapons, traps, and water.

Early in his career Allen reached often for curious metaphors that occasionally seem awkward. Of the thirty-four tropes in the first three chapters of *No Survivors*, this is the most abandoned: ". . . my imagination was already saddled and running full-out again, spurred into a hand-gallop by the magic of my companion's name" (15). Later Allen grew as adept at handling similes and metaphors as Stephen Crane and F. Scott Fitzgerald. A remarkable metaphor occurs in *Return of the Tall Man* when Colonel Clayton, the renegade Civil War veteran turned Sioux, looks with amnesiac hero Ben back in time: "His former life, like Ben Allison's, led only into a box canyon" (61). A grandly indecorous simile comes when the bad heroine of *The Crossing* asks the young hero to help her with her corset strings: "He had no more than touched them, it seemed, when they ran under his hands like a thread raveling out a ripped feed sack" (216).

Literal or figurative, historical or fanciful, serious or guffawing, Henry Allen's style is best remembered for its exhaustless energy. His titles hit the reader hard. Consider *Wolf-Eye, Warbonnet, Tayopa!* He chooses and uses his sources with fierce independence and likes Indian tradition best. His point of view is "hand-close"—or, to quote him again, at least "spit-close"—to the action. The very sounds and smells of his settings rise from his pages, and details stamp authenticity on those pages. His characters stare and glare at you, and speak up, shoot, and gallop along with verve. The action is vigorous, poised, harmonious. Allen's tropes are graphic, outrageous, telling, fun.

Message

Allen does not dramatize a variety of great issues, in the sense that, for example, Owen Wister deplores the changing of old ways, Zane Grey and Ernest Haycox contrast West and East, Walter Van Tilburg Clark deals with the means of justice, A. B. Guthrie, Jr., with killing what we love, or Luke Short with revenge. What Allen does, instead, is to say in effect: It's full? Empty it. You see this coin? Look at its other side. He is bewildering, uniquely contradictory. Just as he uses two pen names, so he is two-handed in presenting aspects of a given Western reality. For example, he writes lovingly about Indians, for their natural nobility, courage, desire for freedom, and reverence for the land; but he also portrays them as savage, often grubby. He regularly fights for the truth, but praises liars and presents contrary sides of many different events. He admires qualities evoked by war but deplores war, especially bad wars. He reveres women but shows men he extols hurting them. Many of his funniest situations and lines are grounded in tragedy or the otherwise lamentable. He often names God in his fiction, but every bit as frequently he both lauds the Red Man for praying to his god (or gods) and also suggests that a force about as powerful as the divine is the successful infernal. Allen seems at times almost Manichean.

The most pervasive subject in Allen is the nineteenth-century Indian. He contrasts Indians sharply, especially the Sioux, Cheyennes, and Apaches. But a careful reading of his works in toto reveals his praise of them all because of their respect for God and nature, and their treatment of land and water, children, the aged, and the insane. His Indians are superb horsemen, warriors, and trail followers. In war they can coordinate action by nothing less than a kind of telepathy; but too often war, being a happy game of gore, evokes their primitivism, individualism, even stupidity. Allen enormously respects Indian instinct, hunches, belief in dreams, keen hearing and telescopic eyesight, bravery, innate courtesy, and steadfastness of both loyalty and enmity. They can shiver you with a stare but avert their gaze when you cry; they are also funny. Among dozens of generalizations about them in Allen, these three are especially useful: Ben Allison thinks about "the Indian way . . . [and] its child-simple chivalry" (*The Tall Men*, 159); then, ". . . that is the way Indians are: make much of nothing and nothing of much" (*From Where the Sun Now Stands*, 185); finally "[t]he Indian is like an iceberg; only one-fifth of his true self shows above the surface. The rest of him lies deep and silent and he does not expose it for any white man, fearing injury, betrayal or death for his trust" (*The Gates of the Mountains*, 189). Reading Allen can reward the attention with innumerable insights concerning the religion, psychology, mores, and living habits of the nineteenth-century Indian. But it is insuperably difficult to draw final conclusions, because, as Allen also generalizes for us through an old Crow spokesman: "'An Indian will always lie... The truth has no hope in it whatever. But an Indian will always tell the truth, also. He just leaves it up to you to understand the difference" (*The Bear Paw Horses*, 177). Meaning no disrespect, I add that Allen is like that Crow.[6]

Nathaniel Hawthorne tells us that we all ought at least to gain something from our inevitable sinning and suffering. William James closes a memorable essay with a statement of approval of this ringing quotation: "'Hang yourself, brave Crillon! We fought at Arques, and you were not there.'"[7] And Ezra Pound carefully distinguishes in "Hugh Selwyn Mauberley" between the bravery of British soldiers in World War I and the lunacies for which they fought. Allen fits right in here. He deplores war but praises the courage, fun, loyalty, camaraderie, and lessons generated therein. A curious proof of this is Fate Beylen's conduct in *San Juan Hill*: he signs up, is obedient and resourceful, and as brave as they come—but declines ever to fire at the enemy. In a remarkable paragraph, Allen has the lad, wounded and almost dead, wonder what it all means. All the fear, misery, carnage, and daring must add up to "the truth" so manifest that "[i]t didn't leave any room for question, any space for uncertainty" (242). When Fate feels the answer inside him, he is at ease. But Allen does not say what the answer is, here. Early in *Black Apache*, however, he does say, when he has his narrator comment on "this wonder of raw courage" displayed by the hero when he fights for others against hopeless odds (49).

Courage is too often directed toward destruction. But love is positive. And Allen repeatedly calls it the best thing in life. The fiery passion of Cetan Mani and Star of the North becomes a memory of the sort that "any man will treasure above all his others on this earth" (*No Survivors*, 93). Kirby Randolph of *Santa Fe Passage* puts it less grandly, but we understand when he opines: "'[T]har ain't really nothin' past a man and his woman'" (119). Allen's finest handling of lovemaking comes in chapter 6 of *The Apache Kid*, when the Kid first is praised for his worship of the land and all natural forces, and then is described as delicately consummating his adoration of his virgin bride not with animality but with "*enthlay-sit-daou*, the old Apache law of iron restraint" (65).

For all his ribaldry, or perhaps by virtue of it, Allen has an opinion of women so high as to amount to an article of faith. He even has

horny Tom Horn aver soberly that "like most cowboys I held a female
to be worth whatever she said she was worth. Happen she was a lady,
she got high respect. Providing she wanted to play, and was still
quality about it, she likewise got treated careful. Was she just a
trampy thing, she would be handled about rougher than a bawly calf
at a branding fire" (*I, Tom Horn,* 268). Perhaps this code contributes
to a pattern in Allen of kisses rough enough to bring blood. On a
more poetic plane, he describes fierce Little Wolf comforting a pregnant squaw. When he asks how the young life within her is growing,
and she replies, " 'Strong! . . . As the seed, so the seedling,' " his
unchauvinistic correction is this: " 'No, Sister, . . . As the soil, so the
sprouting. Remember always that it is the mother who is the earth' "
("Way of the War Chief," in *The Last Warpath,* 179). A canny
old white man in the West voices something similar when he be-
seeches a scared farm woman to trust him, though a stranger: " 'A
woman knows. A woman's not like a man. She feels. She senses things.
I mean past her eyes and ears. You know what I mean, lady? You
believe me?' " ("Sundown Smith," in *The Oldest Maiden Lady in
New Mexico,* 182).

If I had to choose the finest female in all of Allen's works, it
would be Estune of *Chiricahua.* She is beautiful, brave, maternal, resourceful, tough. Her smile "was like a sunrise calm in the autumn-
time, yet smoky and warm. It gave her bronzed face a singular fleeting
beauty" (121). But as terrified readers of *Chiricahua* know, Estune is,
like Mother Nature, more than beautiful.

Allen endorses the concept that physical love can prefigure spiritual
love. It is revenge for loss of the former that initially motivates
Flicker, and constantly the latter that motivates Nunez, in *Black
Apache.* And it is love that binds the two in friendship. In one of
Allen's finest chapters Nunez concludes: "Love is the only mortar
that will cement the soul to salvation" (201).

In Allen's scheme of things God is good, men are a mixture of good
and bad, evil is good at least for being whole and consistent, and
good will win in God's good time if people act heroically. It is no
accident that the last three chapters of the grim novel *The Seven
Men at Mimbres Springs* is dotted with more than a dozen references
to God. Late in *The Feleen Brand* Hush prays, " 'God forgive me for
all I've done' " (175), but, neglecting to follow good prayer with
good deed, is back to rustling two pages later, and thus dooms himself. On the other hand, Mackenna and Francie conclude late in

Mackenna's Gold to abandon the treasure and escape its curse. Their wizened Apache squaw friend agrees: " 'Leave it to God,' she muttered. 'He will take care of it' " (211). Two pages later He does: a *temblor de tierra* buries it. Since everything that rises must converge, prayers to different gods all get to God, whether His name is God, Hunyewat, Maheo, Wakan Tanka, or Yosen. Allen would agree with the following pronouncement by one of his touchstone heroes, Yellowstone Kelly: " 'I have as much respect for the Sioux's Great Spirit as I do for the Catholic's Holy Ghost or the Protestant's Heavenly Father' " (*Yellowstone Kelly*, 15).

". . . Apaches will shrug and grin and say, 'Well, even the white man cannot lie all the time' " (*Chiricahua*, 2). Trying to save his crew from Apache execution, Ben Allison pleads with their captors, " 'How about my friends? One of them is half Sioux.' " The appalling answer?—" 'Other half white. Half white worse than all white' " (*Return of the Tall Man*, 152). Some half-converted Cheyenne kids in *The Day Fort Larking Fell* are discussing religion. One calls the Holy Ghost " 'my favorite. Next to the Devil, anyway,' " he adds; to which another replies, " 'That Devil is hard to beat. He's a fighter, and very crafty. Also, of course, he's an Indian. . . . He's as red as can be' " (163). We can combine elements from these passages, along with many others in Allen, and conclude that he sees good and evil in mortal combat; further, that out-and-out evil is better than hypocrisy; finally, that natural sacrality, with God's help and at His pleasure, will succeed. Over and over Allen tells us not to look back in anguish but forward in hope. He records once, in a late novel, that "[i]mpossible things have a minor habit of happening" (*See How They Run*, 149). A Western novelist as astringent as Henry Wilson Allen will bet on nothing more certain.

As a conclusion to my study of Henry W. Allen's life, fiction, and example, I can hardly do better than quote from a recent essay by Allen entitled "There *Was* an Old West." It has a frosty, autumnal, *ave et vale* tone, for two distinct reasons—old Allen has been wrongly neglected, and he is concerned about the drift that America is taking:

When one who has worked through 30 years and 50 books to protect and preserve it [Allen writes], then comes to that place wherein time bids him say godspeed to the Western Story, what is there for him to set down that will speak truly to the heart of the matter as he has come to know and treasure it in his own lifetime? What canvas can be painted in a few brushstrokes that will reveal his love affair—man, boy, and now old man— with the American West? What poetry can describe the romantic dalliance ensuing with the American Western, that uniquely salt-cured native literature of our vanished frontier past?

And what is this unwanted child of our American storytelling heritage? What is there about the Western that, long-orphaned and roundly disdained by the world of letters, it has survived to become our only original literature?

As well, who are we, the vintners of its thousand myths and legends? We who have toiled all lovingly amid its arid cacti vines to bottle the rawhide wines of the Old West against the day when minstrels may no longer stroll, and the voice of the storyteller fall silent upon the land? What wondrous alchemy of the sagebrush Magi did Ned Buntline bring to his *reductio ad impossibile* of the lore of the American frontier that it has since spread 'round the world to universal popularity? Indeed, that it has since become the glass of critical fashion, the very mold of academic form. Why are respected full professors of English Literature and staid Doctors of American History suddenly mad for what the ruder populace has been acclaiming since Edward Z. C. Judson personally created the Wild West— created it whole, out of the entire cloth of his posturing heroes, vacuous heroines, verdigreed villains and, beyond all, his mythic land and time of their being which itself never existed?

Writers of the Western and the West have "come a far piece" from Judson's dreadful/marvelous dime novels.

The literature of the West has become a serious literature.

College courses are taught upon it and more courses will be taught and more serious scholarship imposed upon the storytellers' original wares. Just here, let the keepers of the Western's watchfires beware. This riskful *abrazo* returns the matter to its positing: What is the Western and why has it survived these hundred-plus years as the people's choice, and now the brand-new pet of the tenured guardians of the Western Word, on campus?

The answer, my friends, is "blowing on the wind." The wind that blows away out there. Away out there "where never is heard a discouraging word, and the skies are not cloudy all day."

The West, friends. That is what the Western is all about.

In the beginning, the Western spelled hope. It held out the West to unnumbered emigrants as the American Hope for a new day and a better life. It is no different today. Through the medium of the American Western, in all its art forms, hope is held forth to any and all the earth around who must believe there is a better day to come and that, if only man be true to himself, there is nothing he cannot dream to conquer.

It is a message, pilgrims. To all men everywhere. Don't give up. Fight

on. Live clean. Be true. Be square. Be fair. You will always win in the end.
You must. It is the Code of the Old West.

But we all know there never was an Old West.

Never could have been, really.

Still, something remains. Something poignant with yesteryears. Red-
olent of mountain red cedar and yellow aspen. Splashing with snow-cold
water. Grand of raw blue sky. Cotton cloud. Woodsmoke adrift in the
valley. Afar the metaled ringing of an ax. The bell of a cow. The alerting
whicker of a pony, nostrils to the wind. The lowing mutter of the herd-
bull up on the bench beyond the fork. A woman's voice calling through
the evening hush. A child's laughter, far away as heaven, near as the heart-
beat it celebrates. Sunset cry of loon on mountain meadow marsh. Sough-
ing of the pines, red with the downing sun. Man at musical chant driving
cattle from the higher grass. . . .

No Old West, you say?

Listen to the cowbell. Smell the cedar incense on the wind. Hear the
axblade sing. Hark to the rider talking down his cattle.

The Old West lives in untold legion of human hearts and minds.

Let it stay there.

Don't ever change it. Cherish its myth, remember the legend, write
down its folklore. Guard it, defend it, keep it safe, that you may pass it
on in your own time as something you want your child to have and to
know as you have had and known it, unspoiled and as a true believer.

Keep the faith, friends; we all know the real truth.

There was an Old West.

There *had* to be.[8]

In an exemplary way Allen has ridden a zigzag course between
sentimentality and cynicism. His voice, humor, diction, subject matter,
themes, message, and example approach one of these extremes or the
other at times, but always avoid them both. Just as he has kept his
eye on the Old West and its best realities in his heart, so we should
treasure his writings.

Notes and References

(Note: Much material in this book derives from my correspondence with Henry W. Allen. References to these letters are noted parenthetically in the text and in the footnotes, in this form: A to G, 9/10/79. The first time I cite a work by Allen, I do so in a footnote; subsequent citations, if any, of the same work will appear parenthetically in the text if the context is clear.)

Chapter One

1. Anne Falke, "Clay Fisher or Will Henry? An Author's Choice of Pen Name," p. 51, in *The Popular Western: Essays Toward a Definition*, eds. Richard W. Etulain and Michael T. Marsden (Bowling Green, Ohio, 1974). Falke's generalization on relative lengths of Henry vs. Fisher novels is not substantiated by the facts. Henry novels average 198 pages; Fishers, 186 pages. (Novels that Allen has published under his own name average 190 pages.) As for relative time spans, dramatic exceptions to Falke's conclusion include the Henry novels *The North Star* (action September and October 1899), *Mackenna's Gold* (July 1897), and especially *The Seven Men at Mimbres Springs* (five days early in April 1861), and the Fisher novels *Yellowstone Kelly* (September 1875 through December 1876) and *The Apache Kid* (1885 until perhaps as late as 1899).

2. Ibid., pp. 52–53.

3. Jon Tuska and Vicki Piekarski, "The Cowboys: New Twists on the Old West," *West Coast Review of Books* 4, no. 6 (1979):74. Tuska recently modified his opinion thus: "...Henry Allen...would be the first to admit that nothing is more misleading than this bifurcation of names, since he has written formulary Westerns as Will Henry and historical reconstructions as Clay Fisher, although his best historical fiction has been published preponderantly under the Will Henry pseudonym"—Jon Tuska, ed., *The American West in Fiction* (New York and Scarborough, Ont.: New American Library, 1982), p. 301.

4. Arnold E. Needham, "Reviews...," *Western American Literature* 1 (Winter 1967):300.

5. A to G, 4/6/82. Allen has repeatedly insisted that he writes for himself rather than with an specific reader or group of readers in mind.

6. Allen to Dale L. Walker (undated); copy sent to me with Allen's permission 10/21/81.

7. Quoted in "Allen, Henry Wilson," *Contemporary Authors*, ed. Frances C. Locher (Detroit, 1980), vols. 89–92, p. 20.

8. A to G, 3/3/81. In A to G, 11/29/81, 12/8/81, Allen suggests that the excursion during which he picked up the attractive hitchhiker occurred in the summer of 1930, after high school and before college.

9. "Allen," *Contemporary Authors*, p. 20.

10. Dust jacket of *To Follow a Flag*; A to G, 7/11/81.

11. A to G, 1/5/81. *Red Blizzard* has not yet been made into a movie. Curiously, Louis L'Amour's first novel, *Westward the Tide* (1950; reprint ed., New York: Bantam Books, 1977), concerns the aftermath of Custer's defeat (as does Allen's *No Survivors* [1950]) and also the legendary Western hero Portugee Phillips (as does Allen's *Red Blizzard* [1951]).

12. A to G, 3/3/81, 2/19/82. "My favorite TV show is the British production of the James Herriot veterinary books, *All Creatures Great and Small*," A to G, 4/20/81.

13. "Allen," *Contemporary Authors*, p. 20.

14. A to G, 12/18/80, 2/15/81, 2/20/81, 7/3/81, 7/23/81, 8/13/81, 8/22/81, 10/7/81.

15. A to G, 1/5/81; ". . . although he [Allen's father] lived several books into my writings of the American West, he never read a line of any of them and always believed that there was still time to get that good job on the [Kansas City] *Star* and so amount to something," quoted in "Allen," *Contemporary Authors*, p. 20.

16. *Roundup* 25 (August 1977):10.

17. A to G, 1/5/81. *The Day the Sun Died*, which was written in 1964 and which Allen allowed me to read, is an account of a Communist Chinese weather-altering plan that miscarries, ices the entire globe, and permits the advance of a Mongolian plan to recolonize all continents once the thaw begins. Only three decent people survive, in Idaho, to thwart the Mongols. The novel is remarkable for its magnificent depiction of arctic America, comic-serious characterizations, brilliant if partly comic-strip plotting, an implicit prediction that after the 1960s American pacificism would surrender most of the Free World, and praise of the old American Indian virtues—specifically, here, Kotzebue Eskimo and Nez Percé ones. Allen still hopes that this novel will be published—A to G, 5/4/83.

18. Most details about the film versions are from Allen Eyles, *The Western* (South Brunswick and New York, 1975).

19. "I did the book in conjunction with Warner Brothers film company, a once-only effort of this nature. They supplied all the research and I wrote the book"—A to G, 6/4/80.

20. *Journey to Shiloh* is Allen's favorite among movies made from his novels—A to G, 2/17/82.

21. Allen calls the movie *Mackenna's Gold* "untrue to the book, miscast, wrongly conceived and executed," "a big budget travesty," and "a disaster"—Allen to Walker (undated), copy to me 10/21/81.

22. Allen brands the script of *Young Billy Young* "obscenely bad"—Allen to Walker (undated), copy to me 10/21/81—and "horrendous"—A to G, 12/8/81.

23. "Frontier's End: Tom Horn," *Time* 115 (June 30, 1980):72. Allen was disgusted with almost everything connected with the movie *Tom Horn*, A to G, 6/11/80. The eight novels sold to the movies but not yet filmed and produced are *Red Blizzard, The North Star, The Blue Mustang, San Juan Hill, The Pitchfork Patrol, The Day the Sun Died, Genesis Five,* and *The Bear Paw Horses*—A to G, 3/3/81. Brian Garfield, the distinguished Western writer and, more recently, film writer and producer, wrote me (3/23/82) that, in his opinion, "Will Henry is unquestionably the best writer alive today who consistently turns or has turned his hand to Westerns."

Chapter Two

1. The excellent 1982 movie *Windwalker*, about a Cheyenne brave who, spared from death to achieve a mission, leaves his funeral platform, may owe something to Allen's *No Survivors*.

2. Will Henry, *No Survivors* (1950; reprint ed., New York: Bantam Books, 1951), p. 80.

3. For background information on Custer and the literary tradition I am indebted to Kent Ladd Steckmesser, *The Western Hero in History and Legend* (Norman: University of Oklahoma Press, 1965), pp. 190–225; and Brian Dippie, *Custer's Last Stand: The Anatomy of an American Myth* (Missoula: University of Montana Press, 1976), pp. 62–68. Since there were no survivors of Custer's Last Stand, authors of fictional accounts of the battle told by white centers of revelation must, according to Dippie, resort to one or more of four plot devices: the fictional survivor can live with the Indians as captive or renegade; he can fight alongside Reno or Benteen; he can carry out Custer's last message; or he can fight beside Custer and unhistorically survive. Strangely, Allen's Colonel Clayton acts in three of these four ways: he is a long-time renegade living with Crazy Horse, aids Reno (and also Captain Thomas B. Weir), and survives not only the last battle but also his own funeral. He even hears Custer's confession of responsibility dictated under fire to his adjutant, Colonel William W. Cooke, shortly before the death of both officers. So Allen's hero amply fulfills Dippie's criteria.

4. The map should be a good one. It derives from one in the *Century Magazine* via Stanley Vestal. See E. S. Godfrey, "Custer's Last Battle, by

One of His Own Troops," *Century Magazine* 43 (n.s. 21) (January 1892):370; and Stanley Vestal, *Warpath and Council Fire* ... (Norman: University of Oklahoma Press, 1948), pp. 238–39.

5. Allen obtained permission of Pocket Books, Inc., his paperback publisher, to sanitize *Red Blizzard* when it was to be reprinted, did so, and was sorry to see the original prose retained verbatim, A to G, 12/12/80. For a chilling fictional treatment of events before and after the Fetterman Massacre, see Michael Straight, *Carrington: A Novel of the West* (New York: Alfred A. Knopf, 1960), published nine years after Allen's *Red Blizzard*.

6. Clay Fisher, *Yellow Hair* (1953; reprint ed., New York: Bantam Books, 1973), p. 17.

7. Allen has his cake and eats it too. He has real-life scout Apache Bill tell Kelso that Custer is a faithful husband and merely enjoyed looking at the gorgeous female interpreter. But Edgar I. Stewart says that the "Cheyenne tradition and legend" to the effect that Mo-nah-see-tah was Custer's mistress and had a son by him is "as reliable as the testimony of anyone else"—Introduction to General George A. Custer, *My Life on the Plains* ... (1874; reprint ed., Norman: University of Oklahoma Press, 1962), p. xx. See also Custer's comments on the Indian girl, especially pp. 282, 365–66.

8. *"Yellowstone Kelly": The Memoirs of Luther S. Kelly*, ed. M. M. Quaife (New Haven: Yale University Press, 1926), p. 141.

9. Clay Fisher, *Yellowstone Kelly* (1957; reprint ed., New York: Bantam Books, 1972), p. vi.

10. Will Henry, *Custer's Last Stand* (1966: reprint ed., New York: Grosset & Dunlap, 1968), p. 42. A contemporary reviewer praised *Custer's Last Stand* for being as accurate as Mari Sandoz's *The Battle of the Little Big Horn* (also 1966) and in addition for conveying a sense of doom effectively—*Library Journal* 91 (November 15, 1966):5760. Allen in "Will Henry and the Indians...," *Roundup* 30 (January 1982):10–11, echoes his Custer's thought and says that he wishes he had been born a High Plains horseback Indian.

11. Clay Fisher, *Warbonnet* (1953; reprint ed., New York: Bantam Books, 1970), p. 150.

12. Clay Fisher, Historical Note, *The Brass Command* (1956; reprint ed., New York: Bantam Books, 1971), no p.

13. William Bird Grinnell, *The Fighting Cheyennes* (1915; reprint ed., Norman: University of Oklahoma Press, 1956), p. 426.

14. These warriors are named Strong Left Hand, Crow, and Wild Hog in Grinnell, *The Fighting Cheyennes*, pp. 418–19.

15. Frederic Remington painted a picture of the final slaughter. See Robert M. Utley and Wilcomb E. Washburn, *The American Heritage*

History of the Indian Wars (New York: American Heritage Publishing Co., 1977), p. 305.

16. Clay Fisher, *The Pitchfork Patrol* (1962; reprint ed., New York: Bantam Books, 1975), no p.

17. The name Nehemiah Bleek is close to that of Nathan Meeker, a real-life Indian agent who flourished later than the time of action in *The Squaw Killers*; Meeker was active during the Colorado-Ute fighting around the White River Agency, 1879. Allen says that Meeker's name did not suggest Bleek's, A to G, 7/3/81.

18. For a recent reprint of contemporary Congressional inquiries into the massacre, see *The Sand Creek Massacre: A Documentary History*, Introduction by John M. Carroll (New York: Sol Lewis, 1973). Especially fascinating are Chivington's testimony (pp. 107–14) and that of Beckwourth (pp. 258–63). Five years before Allen's novel *Maheo's Children*, Michael Straight in his historical novel *A Very Small Remnant* (New York: Alfred A. Knopf, 1963) had also concerned himself with mad Chivington, and stunningly cast Wyncoop as the tragically naïve narrator.

19. Will Henry, *The Squaw Killers* (1968, as *Maheo's Children*; reprint ed., New York: Bantam Books, 1971), p. 31.

20. Will Henry, *The Day Fort Larking Fell* (Philadelphia and New York, 1969), pp. 152, 202. The pageant-like finale resembles a medieval fabliau: pro-Indian white preacher, defecting white lieutenant, enormous pro-Indian white widow, laughing redskin juveniles, and tough dog all caravan out of ruined army fort presided over by uniformed chaos. The end prepares us for a once-projected third novel to feature Preacher Bleek. But Allen abandoned the idea of a Bleek trilogy, A to G, 7/23/81. If William T. Pilkington had considered the humor of *The Day Fort Larking Fell* in his chapter "The Comic Novel in the Southwest," pp. 81–95, in *My Blood's Country: Studies in Southwestern Literature* (Fort Worth: Texas Christian University Press, 1973), he would have found much evidence to which to apply his considerable expertise.

Chapter Three

1. For historical background, see Francis Haines, *The Nez Percés: Tribesmen of the Columbia Plateau* (Norman: University of Oklahoma Press, 1955), pp. 135–36, which cites material familiar to Allen. For recent illustrated-essay coverage of the Steptoe region, see Barbara Austin, "A Paradise Called the Palouse," *National Geographic* 161 (June 1982): 799–818, especially pp. 803, 814.

2. Will Henry, *Pillars of the Sky* (1953, as *To Follow a Flag*; reprint ed., New York: Bantam Books, 1956), p. 110.

3. Unlike Emm, Reuben Bourne in Hawthorne's tale "deserts" his

wounded comrade and returns to the scene of the Indian skirmish too late. Perhaps he should have done what Emm does: he sings "Rock of Ages" to his suffering pal, then shoots him to death.

4. Will Henry, *From Where the Sun Now Stands* (1960; reprint ed., New York: Bantam Books, 1961), p. 230. See also Haines, *The Nez Percés*, p. 280.

5. Tuska and Piekarski rightly call *From Where the Sun Now Stands* "a modern classic of Western American literature"—"The Cowboys," p. 67. Another novel that Allen wrote only after unusually careful historical research is *San Juan Hill*, which includes a bibliography of thirty titles.

6. Modern hikers following Joseph's retreat route will enjoy Daniel Goodenough, Jr., "Lost on Cold Creek," *Montana: The Magazine of Western History* 24 (Autumn 1974):16–29. See also Pascal Tchakmakian, *The Great Retreat: The Nez Perce War in Words and Pictures* (San Francisco: Chronicle Books, 1976); Tchakmakian's description of the Wallowa region (pp. 48, 50) seems influenced by Allen's novel.

7. Here I follow Betty Rosenberg; see her excellent Introduction to Will Henry, *From Where the Sun Now Stands* (Boston: Gregg Press, 1978), pp. vii–viii.

8. Here and elsewhere Allen uses silence as an aspect of modern narrative technique, to relate to his narrators' reflections and speculations; see Robert L. Caserio, *Plot, Story, and the Novel: From Dickens and Poe to the Modern Period* (Princeton: Princeton University Press, 1979), p. 198. For comments on Ernest Haycox's symbolic treatment of silence, see Robert L. Gale, "Ernest Haycox," pp. 188–89, in *Fifty Western Writers*, eds. Richard W. Etulain and Fred Erisman (Westport, Conn.: Greenwood Press, 1982). This valuable reference book is, in my opinion, grievously weakened by the exclusion of Henry W. Allen.

9. Joseph Campbell, *Hero with a Thousand Faces* (1949; reprint ed., Cleveland and New York: World Publishing Co., 1956) throws valuable light on many of Allen's heroes.

10. Will Henry, *The Gates of the Mountains* (1963; reprint ed., New York: Bantam Books, 1967), p. 191.

11. See Campbell, *Hero with a Thousand Faces*, p. 354.

12. See *The Journals of Lewis and Clark*, ed. Bernard DeVoto (Boston: Houghton Mifflin Co., 1953), p. 491. Allen preferred this edition, A to G, 12/18/80. For brief mention of François Rivet see *Original Journals of the Lewis and Clark Expedition 1804–1806 . . .*, ed. Reuben Gold Thwaites (8 vols., 1905; reprint ed., New York: Arno Press, 1969), 1:30, 283, 5:350. See also Harriet D. Munnick, "Francois Rivet," 7:237–43, in *The Mountain Men and the Fur Trade of the Far West . . .*, ed. LeRoy R. Haven (10 vols., Glendale, Calif.: Arthur H. Clark Co., 1965–1972); Donald Jackson, ed., *Letters of the Lewis and Clark Expedition with Related Docu-*

ments 1783–1854 (2d ed., 2 vols., Urbana, Chicago, London: University of Illinois Press, 1978), 1:305n, 2:422, 429n; Harold P. Howard, *Sacajawea* (Norman: University of Oklahoma Press, 1971); David Remley, "Sacajawea of Myth and History," in *Women and Western American Literature*, ed. Helen Winter Stauffer and Susan J. Rosowski (Troy, N.Y.: Whitson Publishing Co., 1982), pp. 70–89. Remley briefly discusses Allen's *The Gates of the Mountains*, for the most part to analyze the dual approach to Sacajawea—beautiful woman, belching squaw—by Rivet, whom Remley oddly calls La Charrette. For a sketch of "The Gate of the Mountains," the Montana gorge "discovered" by Lewis and Clark, see Paul Russell Cutright, *A History of the Lewis and Clark Journals* (Norman: University of Oklahoma Press, 1976), after p. 138. Allen was hard put to it to improve on Vardis Fisher's Lewis and Clark novel *Tale of Valor*, published five years before *The Gates of the Mountains*. *Tale of Valor* hews more closely to the historical line, whereas Allen introduces fictional aspects of Rivet's life with great imaginative skill.

13. For details of real-life John Butterfield's mail service relating to El Paso, see C. L. Sonnichsen, *Pass of the North* (El Paso: Texas Western Press, 1968), pp. 141–53 *passim*.

14. Will Henry, *The Seven Men at Mimbres Springs* (1958; reprint ed., New York: Bantam Books, 1960), p. 113.

15. Mangas Coloradas has been treated fictionally by Will Levington Comfort, in *Apache* (New York: E. P. Dutton & Co., 1931), and Brian Garfield, in *Seven Brave Men* (New York: David McKay & Co., 1966), among others. Allen here owes something to the real-life hole-up of seven men at the Mesilla stage station on July 30, 1861; see Ray Brandes, "Mangas Coloradas: King Philip of the Apache Nation," p. 30, in *Troopers West: Military & Indian Affairs on the American Frontier*, ed. Ray Brandes (San Diego: Frontier Heritage Press, 1970).

16. Clay Fisher, *The Apache Kid* (1961, as *Niño*; reprint ed., New York: Bantam Books, 1973), p. vii. For the Kid's sake I hope that Chuana was not the unattractive Eskiminzin daughter pictured (among other places) in Dan L. Thrapp, *The Conquest of Apacheria* (Norman: University of Oklahoma Press, 1967), after p. 112. Allen may be romanticizing Indians of the Deep Southwest here and elsewhere because, in part, of time-colored recollections of his own half-Navajo cousins: ". . . my mother's brother married two Indian women and had children by each. I met these Indian cousins as a small child, . . . and they fascinated me . . . [w]ith their copper skin, straight blue-black hair, chiseled features and quiet, far-looking manner . . ."—A to G, 12/8/81.

17. Clay Fisher, *Apache Ransom* (New York: Bantam Books, 1974), p. 134.

18. For details concerning Lieutenant Flipper, see *Negro Frontiersman:*

The Western Memoirs of Henry O. Flipper, ed. Theodore D. Harris (El Paso: Texas Western College Press, 1963), pp. 15–20; *The Black Military Experience in the American West*, shorter ed., ed. John M. Carroll (New York: Liveright, 1973), pp. 172–74, 227–32.

19. In an epilogue Allen addresses numerous research problems, calls Eve Ball's *In the Days of Victorio* (Tucson: University of Arizona Press, 1970) fascinating, and quotes from it. Her essay "Juh's Stronghold in Mexico," *Journal of Arizona History* 15 (1974): 73–84, appeared in the same year as Allen's *Apache Ransom*, which is dedicated to Eve Ball.

Chapter Four

1. Josiah Gregg, *Commerce of the Prairies* (New York: H. G. Langley, 1844). There are several later editions. See especially vol. 1, chaps. 2, 3, 4, 5, 6, 12, vol. 2, chaps. 2, 3, 8, 9.

2. Allen may also have been influenced by an amputation scene in Stanley Vestal, *Kit Carson, The Happy Warrior of the Old West: A Biography* (Boston and New York: Houghton Mifflin Co., 1928), pp. 18–22. Kit appears briefly in Allen's *Santa Fe Passage*. Stanley Vestal's *The Santa Fe Trail* (Boston: Houghton Mifflin, Co. 1939), another of Allen's favorite books, may also have proved useful. Following Allen's lead in historomancing, Ben Capps wrote *The Warren Wagontrain Raid* (New York: Dial Press, 1974), an account of Satank, as well as Satanta and Big Tree (both of whom figure in Allen's *Return of the Tall Man*, 1961), their 1871 raid on a Butterfield Trail supply wagon in Texas, and its shameful aftermath.

3. Clay Fisher, *Santa Fe Passage* (1952; reprint ed., New York: Bantam Books, 1953), p. 115.

4. For an account of the feud (with bibliography), see G[ary] L. R[oberts], "Graham-Tewksbury feud (1886–1892)," pp. 455–57, in *The Reader's Encyclopedia of the American West*, ed. Howard R. Lamar (New York, 1977). For detailed treatment, see Harry Sinclair Drago, *The Great Range Wars: Violence on the Grasslands* (New York: Dodd, Mead, 1970), pp. 93–147.

5. Seth Agnew praises Allen's *The Fourth Horseman* thus: "his characters and his creation of the Basin life are thoroughly convincing," in "Cattle for the Couch," *Saturday Review of Literature*, August 14, 1954, p. 12.

6. R. G. Peck, *Chicago Sunday Tribune*, August 26, 1956, p. 4.

7. Clay Fisher, *The Blue Mustang* (1956; reprint ed., New York: Pocket Books, 1957), p. 95.

8. See J. Frank Dobie, *The Mustangs* (New York: Bramhall House, 1952), pp. 273–75.

9. Ibid., p. 274.

10. Will Henry, *The Bear Paw Horses* (1973; reprint ed., New York: Bantam Books, 1973), p. 86. For historical background see James C. Olson, *Red Cloud and the Sioux Problem* (Lincoln: University of Nebraska Press, 1965).

11. In developing his trio of old Crowfoot, his granddaughter Twilight, and white Con Jenkins, Allen modifies the central trio—Kotzebue–Eskimo Toduk, his granddaughter Tanana, and mostly white Tom Camas—from his unpublished novel *The Day the Sun Died* (written in 1964).

12. For Allen's Captain Terrance Smith South, read history's Major Frank J. North; see Donald F. Danker, "The North Brothers and the Pawnee Scouts," *Nebraska History* 42 (September 1961):161–79.

13. See also pp. 201, 207 in *The Bear Paw Horses*. For his comments on "Iktomi," see Stanley Vestal, *The Missouri River* (New York, Toronto: Farrar & Rinehart, 1945), p. 157.

14. For details concerning Story, see Dorothy M. Johnson, *The Bloody Bozeman: The Perilous Trail to Montana Gold* (New York and Toronto: McGraw Hill, 1971), pp. 239–41, 334. A reviewer said of *The Tall Men*: "A mighty good story, but its history is thinner than cigarette paper," *New York Times*, April 11, 1954, p. 33.

15. Clay Fisher, *The Tall Men* (1954; reprint ed., New York: Pocket Books, 1960), p. 74.

16. In a single sentence Allen puts anti-Semitism in its place, when he writes about Esau Lazarus and his support of Stark: "The wise old Jew, sensitive both by gentle nature and the ancient awareness of his race to the persecutions levied upon economic enterprise by a jealous society of spendthrift failures, had from the beginning understood and encouraged the eastern boy's grim determination 'to amount to something' "—Clay Fisher, *The Big Pasture* (1955; reprint ed., New York: Bantam Books, 1972), p. 2.

17. Clay Fisher, *Return of the Tall Man* (1961; reprint ed., New York: Bantam Books, 1971), p. 67.

18. Clay Fisher, *Outcasts of Canyon Creek* (New York: Bantam Books, 1972), p. 164.

19. See Thomas J. Dimsdale, *The Vigilantes of Montana* ... (1866; reprint ed., Ann Arbor; University Microfilms, 1966), pp. 54, 134, 203; and *X. Beidler: Vigilante*, ed. Helen Fitzgerald Sanders (Norman: University of Oklahoma Press, 1957).

Chapter Five

1. When asked about the dog-shooting episode, Allen replied: "The incident has been reported. Killing a dog to prevent apprehension or identification. But I invented the particular old dog to sharpen the point"—A to G, 11/13/81.

2. Will Henry, Author's Note, *The Raiders* (1954, as *Death of a Legend*; reprint ed., New York: Bantam Books, 1956), no p.

3. The Northfield part of *The Long Riders*, the 1980 movie about the James-Younger gang, is as vivid in its way as Allen's description of the original event.

4. When asked about his sources for *The Raiders*, Allen replied: "The Jesse James sources I used were mostly newspaper stories from voluminous clips loaned me by Jesse Woodson James III, of Kansas City, Missouri, my father's best friend in that time and place, and likewise well-known to me..."—A to G, 2/20/81.

5. Reading *Who Rides with Wyatt* in conjunction with Walter Noble Burns's *Tombstone: An Iliad of the Southwest* (Garden City, N.Y.: Doubleday, Doran, 1929), esp. pp. 266–78, may lead one to conclude that Frank Leslie killed Ringo; see also Colin Rickard, " 'Buckskin Frank' Leslie: Gunman of Tombstone," *Southwestern Studies* 2 (Summer 1964):34. Jack Burrows, in "John Ringo: The Story of a Western Myth," *Montana: The Magazine of Western History* 30 (October 1980):2–15, brands as rumor and nonsense the idea that Wyatt killed Ringo, and calls his death suicide.

6. C. L. Sonnichsen, in *From Hopalong to Hud: Thoughts on Western Fiction* (College Station, Texas, and London, 1978), pp. 53–54, chides Allen for linking Wyatt Earp with Nellie Cashman, the probable real-life prototype of Evvie Cushman. Sonnichsen praises *Who Rides with Wyatt* as "a sort of superwestern" (p. 52).

7. A to G, 2/15/81. In *From Hopalong to Hud*, p. 53, Sonnichsen comments about Allen and *Who Rides with Wyatt* thus: "...his work leaves a historically minded reader with mixed feelings. On the one hand he has researched his subjects carefully and takes himself seriously as a historical novelist... On the other hand, he likes to paint in shiny blacks and stark whites, and he gives a tremendous boost to the perpetuation of the [Wyatt Earp] legend." Burrows, in "John Ringo," p. 11, brands Frank Waters's book as "a bitter, inaccurate, and personally intrusive polemic..." Gary L. Roberts, in "The West's Gunmen," *American West* 8 (January 1971):10–15, 64 *passim*, and 8 (March 1971):18–23, 61–62 *passim*, rebukes debunkers in general for handling source material badly.

8. Burns (*Tombstone*, pp. 205, 214) describes Wyatt as "rumbl[ing] savagely" at one point and "lionlike in his magnamity as in his courage" always.

9. "Will Henry/Clay Fisher/Henry W. Allen Books Available for Motion Picture Sale 1/6/80"—unpublished, copy sent to me, A to G, 1/5/81.

10. Will Henry, [prefatory note], *Reckoning at Yankee Flat* (1958; reprint ed., New York: Bantam Books, 1959), no p.

11. When asked, Allen explained that Hush is "not based on any individual. Rather a multiplex story deriving from several real-life Texians of that time [the 1870s]. Afraid I cannot hide behind history (specific) in this one. It's an 'all-original,' as they say"—A to G, 7/3/81.

12. Will Henry, *The Feleen Brand* (New York: Bantam Books, 1962), pp. 178, 177.

13. "George Cassidy" was not called "Butch" until about 1892, after he had worked a while in a butcher shop in Rock Springs, Wyoming—G[ary] L. R[oberts], "Cassidy, Butch," p. 169, in *The Reader's Encyclopedia of the American West.*

14. A to G, 10/7/80. John Rolfe Burroughs, to whom Allen refers here, is the author of *Where the Old West Stayed Young* (New York, 1962; reprint ed., New York, n.d.), which is largely about Brown's Hole, is probably Allen's favorite nonfictional work, and is certainly the inspiration of much of his finest writing.

15. Harry Longbaugh (or Longabaugh), better known as the Sundance Kid, does not appear in *Alias Butch Cassidy*, which was published two years before the popular 1969 movie *Butch Cassidy and the Sundance Kid* was released.

16. To compare the nearly identical descriptions, see Will Henry, *Alias Butch Cassidy* (1967; reprint ed., New York: Bantam Books, 1969), p. 129, and Will Henry, *One More River to Cross* (1967; reprint ed., New York: Bantam Books, 1969), pp. 75–76.

17. Allen has expressed sadness that almost no black readers have written him to voice appreciation: "Very few if any western novelists have done serious books about a black hero; I've done two ... and have also used blacks frequently and favorably in my other books.... I have heard from precisely one black in all the years"—A to G [5/6/81].

18. For details, see Burroughs, *Where the Old West Stayed Young*, pp. 205–8, 210–11, 214.

19. See Tom Horn, *Life of Tom Horn* ... (1904; reprint ed., with Introduction by Dean Krakel [Norman: University of Oklahoma Press, 1964]), pp. 213–25.

20. "I swear I never heard of 'Owl Creek Bridge' until you mentioned it"—A to G, 10/13/80. Allen expresses satisfaction with *I, Tom Horn* thus: "... I can't write a great deal better than I did in the Tom Horn book"—A to G, 1/1/81. But of the 1980 movie adaptation, called *Tom Horn* and starring Steve McQueen, Allen writes: "I ... did the first screenplay from the book, my book, that is. McQueen didn't like it and subsequently went through seven screenwriters before coming up with the final shooting script. I read it and it was awful. I hear the film is likewise. Wouldn't doubt it.... In process of the film's final editing, I brought Mc-

Queen to Guild arbitration over title credits. I lost, and Solar Productions took my name off the picture. Perhaps they did me a favor"—A to G, 6/11/80.

21. See Jon Tuska, "The American West in Fiction, Part II," *Roundup* 29 (June 1981):24–28 *passim*; Gordon D. Shirreffs, "Lee Kershaw's 'Mana': Not Guilty," *Roundup* 29 (September–October 1981):9–12; and J. T. Edson, [letter], *Roundup* 29 (September–October 1981):29.

22. Will Henry, *I, Tom Horn* (1975; reprint ed., New York: Bantam Books, 1975), p. 153.

23. Eugene Cunningham, *Triggernometry: A Gallery of Gunfighters* (New York: The Press of the Pioneers, 1934), pp. 359–88; see also Krakel, Introduction, *Life of Tom Horn*, pp. x–xii.

Chapter Six

1. For a convenient historical account of military and allied events bearing on *The Crossing*, see Howard Roberts Lamar, *The Far Southwest: 1846–1912: A Territorial History* (New Haven: Yale University Press, 1966), pp. 110–21.

2. Clay Fisher, *The Crossing* (1958; reprint ed., New York: Bantam Books, 1974), p. 121.

3. See Robert L. Kerby, *The Confederate Invasion of New Mexico and Arizona 1861–1862* (Los Angeles: Westernlore Press, 1958), p. 88; Martin Hardwick Hall, *Sibley's New Mexico Campaign* (Austin: University of Texas Press, 1960), pp. 185, 198.

4. Will Henry, *Journey to Shiloh* (1960; reprint ed., New York: Bantam Books, 1963), p. 4.

5. Dale L. Walker, author of *Death Was the Black Horse: The Story of Rough Rider "Buckey" O'Neill* (Austin: Madrona Press, 1975), greatly admires Allen's *San Juan Hill*. Walker wrote me (2/2/82) in part thus: "I loved and admired Will's handling of Buckey and I still do, after writing Buckey's life. . . . Will's characterization of Theodore Roosevelt is absolutely superb, the best in all fiction, in my opinion. . . . Also, it takes a man of Will Henry's humor to do a proper job on the Rough Riders. . . . Fate Beylen is an excellent exemplar of the territorial cowboy that made up that portion of the 1st. U.S. Volunteer Cavalry."

6. A more awful pun appears in a soldier's response when Buck Burnett in *Journey to Shiloh* apologizes for griping at the loss of his left arm: " 'Hell, you got a right' " (137).

7. Will Henry, *San Juan Hill* (1962; reprint ed., New York: Bantam Books, 1965), p. 111.

8. Allen reports that "*Smoke* was the title of the French hardcover edition of *The North Star*. I guess they . . . liked the dog"—A to G, 1/15/81.

9. Will Henry, *The North Star* (1956; reprint ed., New York: Bantam Books, 1958), p. 79.

10. See J. Frank Dobie, *Apache Gold & Yaqui Silver* (Boston, 1939), pp. 3–148, 185–259, 289–307. Allen dedicated *Tayopa!* to Dobie.

11. Will Henry, *Mackenna's Gold* (1963; reprint ed., New York: Bantam Books, 1966), p. 66.

12. Similarities between Allen's novels of lost gold mines in Apacheria and B. Traven's 1927 masterpiece *The Treasure of the Sierra Madre* are of interest. Both novelists consider the rapacity of Spanish rulers and Catholic churchmen in Mexico. Both warn that the lure of gold brings out forbidden impulses in men. Both suggest that Mother Nature's body should not be ripped open to expose gold, which is an illusory treasure. And both say that a better treasure than gold is learning to care for others.

13. Historian Bernal Diaz describes Hernando Cortes's reception by and treatment of Montezuma in the city of Mexico. Nineteenth-century Porfirio Diaz did better by Mexico. Dobie mentions both in *Apache Gold & Yaqui Silver*, pp. 165, 203.

14. Ibid., pp. 191–93.

15. Henry W. Allen, *Tayopa!* (New York: Pocket Books, 1970), pp. 6ff.

16. Dobie, in *Apache Gold & Yaqui Silver*, pp. 193–94, says that Nàcori is probably near the site of the Tayopa mine.

17. In ibid., pp. 203–10, 232, Dobie connects Henry Ossian Flipper, model of Allen's Robert E. Lee Flicker, to the Tayopa mine. Flipper was evidently not concerned with El Naranjal.

18. Clay Fisher, *Black Apache* (New York: Bantam Books, 1974), p. 87.

19. The development of the love theme, as well as the style, in *Black Apache* makes it reminiscent of Wilder's 1927 novel.

Chapter Seven

1. Clay Fisher, *The Oldest Maiden Lady in New Mexico and Other Stories* (New York: Macmillan Co., 1962), p. 17.

2. Allen writes about Cole's good deed thus: "The story of his softness with the little girl in the bloodied Northfield retreat is mine own tale, ... an invention to put the maximum point on the pencil"—A to G, 11/13/81. Allen converted "Sundown Smith," "The Hunting of Tom Horn," and "A Mighty Big Bandit" into three successful television scripts, all in 1959. The first was for the *Zane Grey Theatre*, and the other two were for *Tales of Wells Fargo*—A to G, 3/3/81.

3. Allen's converting of segments from earlier novels into later short stories is a vexing critical problem. When I wrote Allen about it, he replied: "I share your trouble with short stories which are taken verbatim

from the text of a writer's novels. I understood this onus when I first made the choice to burden myself with it. My argument was that the general reader would never know the difference. He would enjoy the purloined bit without a moment's spoiling of spying out where it had come from. If there is a touch of larcenous whitewash in that view, . . . it is also somewhat of an innocent advantage-taking of the reader. . . . It disturbs me, yes. But I remain thinking it is 'relatively' an innocent crime. Ninety-five percent of the readers of these excerpted stories will not know the difference . . . Except, perhaps, in that the reader may tend to find the excerpted stories better . . ."—A to G, 7/3/81.

4. Will Henry, *The Last Warpath* (1966; reprint ed., New York: Bantam Books, 1967), p. 67. Blunt's harangue against mixed blood is contrary to a statement Allen published a year earlier, in which an old Cheyenne tells a Mandan boy with blood in him from York, the Lewis and Clark expedition black: " 'To bear mixed blood is a blessing, not a curse, for straight blood runs narrow in the veins' "—Will Henry, *In the Land of the Mandans* (Philadelphia and New York: Chilton Books, 1965), p. 18.

5. Did Allen keep all of this genealogical matter scrupulously straight? No. He reports early that Whistling Elk was the son of Lighting Swan and Far Hills Elk (9) but later that Whistling Elk was the husband of Lighting Swan and that the two were the parents of Spotted Wolf (240). I assume that the latter information is erroneous and that Spotted Wolf was really the grandson of Lighting Swan and Far Hills Elk, who had a son named Spotted Wolf, who had a daughter named Moheya. Allen is in good company: William Faulkner also confused his fictive genealogy a time or two. *The Last Warpath* treats many Cheyenne generations. Actually, it includes legends told to Goodfeather by her grandmother, who is thus Moheya's great-great-great-great-great-grandmother!

6. Will Henry, *Sons of the Western Frontier*, vol. 1, *Red Brother and White* (1966; reprint ed., New York: Bantam Books, 1969), p. 16.

7. Allen says that he submitted a handwritten draft of this story to *Liberty* magazine when he was eleven years old, but it was rejected. He sold it forty-three years later. "Title and text [he adds] were substantially unchanged from the eleven-year old boy's concept. They were only 'adultized' to look professional. Which goes to show I am sure that writers are born, not manufactured, and they should never throw anything away"—A to G, 12/8/81.

8. When asked whether Asaph was Billy the Kid's father, Allen replied: "I'm not sure how I saw Asaph in terms of actually fathering the Child Bonney. Perhaps it was more the idea of him invading the child at birth. Then again, why did I first call the original blank verse version Asaph's Seed? Perhaps, well, *Quien Sabe?*"—A to G, 7/23/81.

9. Will Henry, Introduction to *14 Spurs* (New York: Bantam Books, 1968), p. ix.

10. Will Henry, *The Texas Rangers* (New York: Random House, 1957), p. 122.

11. "Good writing, strength, and honest sensitivity combine to make this animal story one of unique poignancy"—*Kirkus* 26 (August 1, 1958): 549.

12. Clay Fisher, *Valley of the Bear* (Boston: Houghton Mifflin Co., 1964), p. 21.

13. Will Henry, *In the Land of the Mandans* (Philadelphia and New York, 1965), p. 137.

14. Henry W. Allen, *See How They Run* (New York: Pocket Books, 1970), p. 171.

15. In making Yang Suntar a mutant, Allen is following a hoary science-fiction tradition; see Darko Suvin, *Metamorphoses of Science Fiction: On the Poetics and History of a Literary Genre* (New Haven: Yale University Press, 1979), p. 201.

16. Henry W. Allen, "Guarding the Packline to the Past," *Roundup* 29 (May 1981):6.

17. "Will Henry and the Indians By the author of *From Where the Sun Now Stands* As told to Henry W. Allen," *Roundup* 30 (January 1982):12.

Chapter Eight

1. Obviously the children's books Allen wrote have juvenile points of view, although none uses first-person narration.

2. For an analysis of one aspect of this trick, see Ralf Norrman, "End-Linking as an Intensity-Creating Device of Henry James's *The Golden Bowl*," *English Studies* 61 (1980):236–51.

3. *The Squaw Killers* falls into nicely unequal quarters, of fifteen, eleven, fifteen, and eleven chapters respectively.

4. Pp. 8, 26, 32, 66, 107. Many poker images appear also in *The Fourth Horseman*. The entire foreword of Clay Fisher, *Nine Lives West* (New York: Bantam Books, 1978), is a poker metaphor. Craps was never Allen's game, to judge from his use of only one dice image—see *San Juan Hill*, p. 40.

5. See especially pp. 8–9, 15, 67, 94, 193.

6. A Canadian reader telephoned Allen in November 1981 to thank him for advancing the philosophy that "[t]he truth has no hope in it." The fan "said the passage had roused him from despair, given him a grasp on life, a handle to hold to that would permit him to keep on, would give him a perspective for seeing the world the way it was, thus coping with it"—A to G, 11/10/81.

7. William James, "Is Life Worth Living?", in *The Will to Believe and Other Essays in Popular Philosophy* (1897; reprint ed., New York: Dover Publications, 1956), p. 62.

8. Henry Wilson Allen, "There *Was* an Old West," *Roundup* 31 (April 1983):9–10.

Selected Bibliography

PRIMARY SOURCES

(In order of publication. The abbreviation WH in parentheses after a title means by Will Henry, CF means Clay Fisher, HWA means Henry Wilson Allen. Numbers on map [in chronological order] correspond to numbers in parentheses after some book titles, to locate the main or climactic setting of the work.)

1. Novels

No Survivors (WH, 1). New York: Random House, 1950; New York: Bantam Books, 1951.

Red Blizzard (CF, 2). New York: Simon & Schuster, 1951; New York: Pocket Books, Inc., 1953.

Santa Fe Passage (CF, 4). Boston and New York: Houghton Mifflin, 1952; New York: Bantam Books, 1953.

To Follow a Flag (WH, 5). New York: Random House, 1953; New York: Bantam Books, as *Pillars of the Sky*, 1956.

Yellow Hair (CF, 6). Boston and New York: Houghton Mifflin, 1953; New York: Bantam Books, 1973.

Warbonnet (CF, 7). Boston and New York: Houghton Mifflin, 1953; New York: Bantam Books, 1970.

The Fourth Horseman (WH, 8). New York: Random House, 1954; New York: Bantam Books, 1956.

Death of a Legend (WH, 9). New York: Random House, 1954; New York: Bantam Books, as *The Raiders*, 1956.

The Tall Men (CF, 10). Boston and New York: Houghton Mifflin, 1954; New York: Pocket Books, 1960.

Who Rides with Wyatt (WH, 11). New York: Random House, 1955; New York: Bantam Books, 1956.

The Big Pasture (CF, 12). Boston and New York: Houghton Mifflin, 1955; New York: Bantam Books, 1972.

The North Star (WH). New York: Random House, 1956; New York: Bantam Books, 1958.

The Blue Mustang (CF, 13). Boston and New York: Houghton Mifflin, 1956; New York: Pocket Books, 1957.

The Brass Command (CF, 14). Boston and New York: Houghton Mifflin, 1956; New York: Bantam Books, 1971.

Pillars of the Sky, 1956. See *To Follow a Flag*, 1953, above.

The Raiders, 1956. See *Death of a Legend*, 1954, above.

Yellowstone Kelly (CF, 15). Boston and New York: Houghton Mifflin, 1957; New York: Bantam Books, 1972.

Reckoning at Yankee Flat (WH, 17). New York: Random House, 1958: New York: Bantam Books, 1959.

The Seven Men at Mimbres Springs (WH, 18). New York: Random House, 1958; New York: Bantam Books, 1960.

The Crossing (CF, 19). Boston and New York: Houghton Mifflin, 1958; New York: Bantam Books, 1974.

From Where the Sun Now Stands (WH, 20). New York: Random House, 1960; New York: Bantam Books, 1961.

Journey to Shiloh (WH, 21). New York: Random House, 1960; New York: Bantam Books, 1963.

Niño (CF, 22). New York: William Morrow, 1961; New York: Bantam Books, as *The Apache Kid*, 1973.

Return of the Tall Man (CF, 23). New York: Pocket Books, 1961; New York: Bantam Books, 1972.

San Juan Hill (WH). New York: Random House, 1962; New York: Bantam Books, 1965.

The Feleen Brand (WH, 24). New York: Bantam Books, 1962.

The Pitchfork Patrol (CF, 25). New York: The Macmillan Co., 1962; New York: Bantam Books, 1975.

Mackenna's Gold (WH, 26). New York: Random House, 1963; New York: Bantam Books, 1966.

The Gates of the Mountains (WH, 27). New York: Random House, 1963; New York: Bantam Books, 1966.

Custer's Last Stand (WH, 29). Philadelphia and New York: Chilton Book Co., 1966; New York: Grosset & Dunlap Tempo Books, 1968.

Alias Butch Cassidy (WH, 30). New York: Random House, 1967; New York: Bantam Books, 1969.

One More River to Cross (WH, 31). New York: Random House, 1967; New York: Bantam Books, 1969.

Maheo's Children (WH, 32). Philadelphia and New York: Chilton Book Co., 1968; New York: Bantam Books, as *The Squaw Killers*, 1971.

Genesis Five (HWA). New York: William Morrow, 1968; New York: Pyramid Books, 1970.

The Day Fort Larking Fell (WH, 33). Philadelphia and New York: Chilton Book Co., 1969.

Tayopa! (HWA, 34). New York: Pocket Books, 1970.

See How They Run (HWA). New York: Pocket Books, 1970.

The Squaw Killers, 1971. See *Maheo's Children*, 1968, above.

Chiricahua (WH, 35). Philadelphia and New York: J. B. Lippincott, 1972; New York: Bantam Books, 1973.

Outcasts of Canyon Creek (CF, 36). New York: Bantam Books, 1972.

The Bear Paw Horses (WH, 37). Philadelphia and New York: J. B. Lippincott, 1973; New York: Bantam Books, 1973.

The Apache Kid, 1973. See *Niño*, 1961, above.

Apache Ransom (CF, 38). New York: Bantam Books, 1974.

I, Tom Horn (WH, 39). Philadelphia and New York: J. B. Lippincott, 1975; New York: Bantam Books, 1975.

Black Apache (CF, 40). New York: Bantam Books, 1976.

Summer of the Gun (WH, 41). Philadelphia and New York: J. B. Lippincott, 1978; New York: Bantam Books, 1979.

2. Short-Story Collections

The Oldest Maiden Lady in New Mexico and Other Stories (CF). New York: The Macmillan Co., 1962. Contains "The Oldest Maiden Lady in New Mexico," "King Fisher's Road," "The Redeeming of Fate Rachel," "Pretty Face," "The Chugwater Run," "Sundown Smith," "The Hunting of Tom Horn," "A Mighty Big Bandit," "Isley's Stranger," "The Deputization of Walter Mendenhall," "Ghost Town," "The Trap."

The Last Warpath (WH). New York: Random House, 1966; New York: Bantam Books, 1967. Contains "The Pale Eyes," "Little Dried River," "Half-Blood Brother," "Red Runs the Washita," "Peace of the Pony Soldiers," "Way of the War Chief," "Maheo's Children," "The Last Warpath."

Sons of the Western Frontier (WH). Philadelphia and New York: Chilton Book Co., 1966; New York: Bantam Books, 1969. *Red Brother and White* (vol. 1 of *Sons of the Western Frontier*) contains "The Friendship of Red Fox," "Second Chance to Santa Fe," "River of Decision," "Legend of Trooper Hennepin," "Lapwai Winter." *Outlaws and Legends* (vol. 2 of *Sons of the Western Frontier*) contains "Vengeance of Jesse James," "Rough Riders of Arizona," "Ghost Wolf of Thunder Mountain," "A Bullet for Billy the Kid," "Bandits of Tehuantltux," "The Tallest Indian in Toltepec."

Red Brother and White, 1969. See *Sons of the Western Frontier*, 1966, above.

Outlaws and Legends, 1969. See *Sons of the Western Frontier*, 1966, above.

Nine Lives West (CF). New York: Bantam Books, 1978. Partly a reprint of stories from *The Oldest Maiden Lady in New Mexico and Other Stories*, 1962—see above. Contains "A Mighty Big Bandit," "The Streets of Laredo," "The Skinning of Black Coyote," "For Want of a Horse," "The Redeeming of Fate Rachel," "King Fisher's Road," "The Trap," "The Hunting of Tom Horn," "Sundown Smith."

Seven Legends West (CF). New York: Bantam Books, 1983. Partly a reprint of stories from *The Oldest Maiden Lady in New Mexico and Other Stories*, 1962—see above. Contains "The Deputization of Walter Mendenhall," "Pretty Face," "The Oldest Maiden Lady in New Mexico," The Chugwater Run," "The White Man's Road," "The Rescue of Chuana," "Isley's Stranger."

Will Henry's West. Introduction by Dale L. Walker. El Paso: Texas Western Press, 1984. Reprinted and new essays and stories.

3. Children's Books

Wolf-Eye: The Bad One (WH, 3). New York: Julian Messner, 1951.

The Texas Rangers (WH, 16). New York: Random House Landmark Books, 1957.

Orphan of the North (WH). New York: Random House, 1958.

Valley of the Bear (CF). Boston and New York: Houghton Mifflin, 1964.

In the Land of the Mandans (WH, 28). Philadelphia and New York: Chilton Books, 1965.

4. Critical Essays

Introduction. *14 Spurs: Western Writers of America* (ed. WH). New York: Bantam Books, 1968.

"Breaking Ground for a Novel" (HWA). *Roundup* 21 (September 1973):12–13, 15.

"Guarding the Packline to the Past" (HWA). *Roundup* 29 (May 1981): 5–8.

"The Far-out West" (HWA). *South Dakota Review* 19 (Spring/Summer 1981):114–25.

"Will Henry and the Indians By the Author of *From Where the Sun Now Stands* As told to Henry W. Allen" (HWA). *Roundup* 30 (January 1982):9–13.

"There *Was* an Old West" (HWA). *Roundup* 31 (April 1983):9–10.

5. Unpublished Materials

The Day the Sun Died (WH—novel [1964]).

"Will Henry/Clay Fisher/Henry W. Allen Books Available for Motion Picture Sale 1/6/80" (HWA).

SECONDARY SOURCES

1. Books

Burroughs, John Rolfe. *Where the Old West Stayed Young.* 1962; reprint ed., New York: Bonanza Books, n.d. About Brown's Hole. One of Allen's favorite source books.

Dobie, J. Frank. *Apache Gold & Yaqui Silver.* Boston: Little, Brown & Co., 1939. Another of Allen's favorite source books. Allen dedicated his *Tayopa!* to Dobie.

Durham, Philip, and Jones, Everett L. *The Negro Cowboys.* New York: Dodd, Mead, 1965. Discusses black cowboys and their contributions from Texas to Montana. Allen dedicated his *Chiricahua* to Durham and Jones.

Eyles, Allen. *The Western.* South Brunswick and New York: A. S. Barnes, 1975. Includes mention of most of the movies made to date from Allen novels.

Gale, Robert L. *Will Henry/Clay Fisher.* Boise, Idaho: Boise State University Press Western Writers Series, 1982. Reliable brief coverage.

Lamar, Howard R., ed. *The Reader's Encyclopedia of the American West.* New York: Thomas Y. Crowell Co., 1977. Useful in a thousand ways.

Locher, Frances C., ed. "Allen, Henry Wilson." In *Contemporary Authors,* vols. 89–92, pp. 19–20. Detroit: Gale Research, 1980. Contains basic biographical information, much in Allen's own words.

Nye, Russel. *The Unembarrassed Muse: The Popular Arts in America.* New York: Dial Press, 1970. Surveys the development of Western literature; praises Allen briefly.

Sonnichsen, C. L. *From Hopalong to Hud: Thoughts on Western Fiction.* College Station, Texas, and London: Texas A & M University Press, 1978. Contains separate essays; mentions Allen tangentially.

Tuska, Jon. "Allen, Henry Wilson." In *Twentieth-Century Western Writers,* ed. James Vinson (Detroit: Gale Research, 1982), pp. 20–24. Describes the versatility of Allen and then wrongly criticizes him for it.

2. Articles

"'All Time' Best Westerns Roster Is WWA Release." *Roundup* 25 (August 1977):10. Names *From Where the Sun Now Stands* as one of the twenty-five best westerns of all time, with *I, Tom Horn* as one of the five runners-up.

Falke, Anne. "Clay Fisher or Will Henry? An Author's Choice of Pen Name." In *The Popular Western: Essays Toward a Definition,* ed.

Richard W. Etulain and Michael T. Marsden, pp. 50–58. Bowling Green, Ohio: Bowling Green University Popular Press, 1974. Attempts to distinguish between Fisher novels and Henry novels.

Index

(The works of Henry W. Allen [HWA], Clay Fisher [CF], and Will Henry [WH] are all listed under Allen, Henry Wilson)